The Something-Went-Wrong-What-Do-I-Do-Now Cookbook

The
Something-Went-Wrong-
What-Do-I-Do-Now
Cookbook

*What to do
about salty soup,
burned stew, fallen
cakes, overcooked cauli-
flower, runny eggs, crusty
pots, and hundreds
of other kitchen
catastrophes*

by
John and Marina Bear

Drawings by Roy Doty

Harcourt Brace Jovanovich, Inc., New York

First edition

ISBN 0-15-183735-X

LIBRARY OF CONGRESS CATALOG CARD NUMBER: 79-117569

Printed in the United States of America

To our mothers,

Tina Klempner and Mary Dorrow,

whose cooking has been an inspiration

If this is coffee, please bring me some tea;
but if this is tea, please bring me some coffee.
—ABRAHAM LINCOLN

Contents

The Something-Went-Wrong-What-Do-I-Do-Now Cookbook

Introduction

There are thousands of cookbooks in the world, and they are all, at heart, the same.

They tell you how to cook.

This book is different.

It tells you what to do when something goes wrong. It tells you how to correct mistakes. It tells you how to undo whatever it is you have done that you did not *want* to have done. It tells you what to do about fallen cakes, salty soups, burned stews, over-cooked cauliflower, and hundreds of other things that can happen even to the best of cooks.

Read the preface or introduction to your favorite cookbook. The chances are you'll find a paragraph something like this:

IMPORTANCE OF FOLLOWING INSTRUCTIONS

Each recipe in this book has been carefully tested and checked for accuracy. It is important that you follow instructions *exactly*.

Be sure you measure ingredients *carefully,* and time your cooking *precisely.* This is the only way you can guarantee perfect results every time.

Fine. We agree. Makes lots of sense.

But among all those thousands of cookbooks, there is not a single one that tells you what to do when:

1. The doorbell rings, and while you're paying postage due to the mailman, the cauliflower overcooks and turns yellow and mushy.

2. You're not wearing your glasses, and you set the burner too high, and the baked beans have burned.

3. The cheese you were going to put in the casserole has gone moldy.

4. The telephone rings while you're making the gravy, and by the time you get back, it's all lumpy (the gravy, not the telephone).

5. The only loaf of bread in the house is stale, and the school bus is due soon, and you have to make those sandwiches for the kids.

6. The stew is simmering away, and you sample it, and it tastes more like K-rations than *boeuf bourguignon.*

7. You put salt in the vegetable soup and forget you did and put it in again, and now it's much too salty.

8. Your invitation said dinner promptly at seven, and it's after six and you find you didn't put the potatoes in with the roast.

9. They had this fantastic special at the store, and you went mad, and now you have five heads of lettuce sitting there wilting.

10. Your husband unexpectedly brings his boss home for dinner, and there just won't be enough chicken to go around.

And so on. And so on. And so on.

In other words, none of the other cookbooks tell you how to correct mistakes. None of them tell you how to undo the damage that you (or the supermarket or Mother Nature or the cow) have already done.

4

This book does.

This book tells you what to do when you discover that just about any kind of food, drink, or utensil is overcooked, undercooked, stale, spoiled, burned, lumpy, salty, peppery, bland, too spicy, too hot, too cold, moldy, frozen, gamy, fuzzy, mushy, too dry, too wet, flat, tough, too thick, too thin, wilted, fatty, collapsed, exploded, shriveled, curdled, cracked, scaly, smelly, greasy, dirty, stringy, twiggy, mealy, clogged, or stuck together.

This book is *The Something-Went-Wrong-What-Do-I-Do-Now Cookbook.*

Note in Passing

In the preparation of this book, we looked at more than 2,000 different cookbooks, to see if any of them paid special attention to correcting mistakes. None did. All of them, we found, can be divided into only five basic categories.

First, there are the Businesslike Cookbooks. They have businesslike titles, like *Basic Culinary Techniques,* or *Mrs. Rutherford's Cooking Academy Cookbook.* They simply tell you how to cook. *And they seem to assume nothing will ever go wrong.*

Second, there are the Specialized Cookbooks. *The Cranberry Cookbook. The Parsnip Cookbook. Antarctican Cookery. 96,001 Tempting Recipes for Leftover Okra.* But all they do is tell you how to cook cranberries. Or parsnips. Or penguins. Or whatever. Never what to do if something goes wrong.

Third, there are the Expensive Gimmicky Cookbooks, made solely to be given as gifts. No one has ever been known to buy one for herself. Books like *Favorite Recipes of All the Postmasters*

General. Or *Secrets of Babe Ruth's Kitchen.* These books don't help you when anything goes wrong—unless you can be consoled looking at the magnificent full-color glossy photographs of tomatoes and onion slices and roast beefs.

Fourth, there are the Anecdotal Cookbooks, which tend to be travel books, joke books, and/or autobiographies, with recipes thrown in. *Through Darkest Peru with Sterno and Toothpick.* *Take It Off, Take It Off (It's Boiling Over),* the warm witty story of Flame LaFleur, Queen of Burlesque and Queen of the Kitchen. Anecdotes aside, these books tell you how to cook. But never what to do when something goes wrong.

And finally there is the unending flow of Folksy Cookbooks, in which someone has *finally* persuaded Aunt Bessie or Mrs. Mugglesby of Sunny Shadows Farm to record for posterity all their famous receipts (which is the folksy word for recipe). So we have *Aunt Bessie's Own Cookbook,* and *The Eatin's Good on Sunny Shadows Farm.* Presumably Aunt Bessie never made mistakes. If she did, she ain't talkin'.

How This Book Is Organized

The major part of the book consists of an alphabetical listing of all foods and then, under each specific food, an alphabetical listing of things that might go wrong, along with how they can be corrected.

For example, we have:

ASPARAGUS
Bland
Frozen to box
Not enough
Old
Overcooked
Salty
Thawed
Too much

Of course the subcategories will differ for each food; no two foods have an identical array of potential problems. Some problems you run into may simply not be listed. There is a good reason: Not every problem has a solution—or has, in fact, been identified. Who knows, you may be the first person in the whole world suffering from stringy hamburgers. We hope that as more and more people get intrigued with the idea of the philosophy of this book, future editions will report their problems—and their (or our) ingenious solutions.

So, will you send us your problems, questions, suggestions, solutions—everything but the kitchen sink (and that, too, if there's something wrong with it)? Write to John and Marina Bear, c/o Harcourt Brace Jovanovich, Inc., 757 Third Avenue, New York, New York 10017. And thank you.

When you *don't* find the answer to your problem in this book, it behooves you to improvise, bluff, or otherwise muddle through. To assist you when the need arises—and it will, it will—we have included a brief section entitled "How to Improvise, Bluff, or Otherwise Muddle Through." Here you will find some general philosophy, along with a list of basic ingredients for a kitchen "first-aid kit"—foods that can be used in different ways to help solve a variety of problems.

Also, there are some corrective techniques that apply not to a single specific food or problem, but to a wide range of foods. For instance, there are things you can do about burned foods that work equally well with burned cauliflower, burned stew, or burned pudding. The same is true for frozen foods that have thawed out before you wanted them to. So, for advice relevant to these two situations—burning and thawing—see Appendixes A and B at the back of the book.

There are other appendixes back there, too, dealing with measuring, pouring, seasonability of foods, stain removal, and so forth. Each is described briefly on the Contents page.

Appendix H deserves special mention. It is called "Problems with Utensils" and deals with situations ranging from burned pots to clogged grinders. It even covers those handy utensils you carry around with you on the ends of your arms: what to do about burned, greasy, smelly, and stained hands.

One more thing.

Into every cook's life there comes Total Failure.

Sometimes twice a week.

Total Failure is a different kind of situation from any of the others we discuss. So we have given it a special section, just before the start of the alphabetical listing.

We hope you'll never need to use this book—in much the same way we hope you'll never need to see a doctor. But we hope you will agree, in both cases, that you're kind of glad they're there.

How to Improvise, Bluff,
or Otherwise Muddle Through

This is the Great Encouragement chapter. The one you refer to when the main course has turned blue; when the dessert hasn't jelled yet; when there's a funny smell in the front hall and you discover it is coming from the oven.

Or, more specifically, come back to these pages when you have a specific problem that isn't covered in the main part of the text.

Our message is, Take heart! When everything seems to be going wrong—or *has* in fact gone wrong—it is still possible to snatch victory (and your dinner) from the very jaws of defeat (and the garbage pail). You need only courage, a bit of creativity (yours or ours), and a good set of "first-aid" ingredients for repairing or doctoring injured food.

Here, then, is a list of emergency supplies that should equip you to weather a wide variety of kitchen catastrophes. And in case *everything* goes wrong, it is even possible to create an entire gourmet meal out of nothing more than these ingredients. See Appendix F for details.

FIRST-AID SUPPLIES

One box of dried onions. No one ever expects to run out of fresh onions. Everyone does at least 4.7 times per year. Dried onions are a natural for helping to fill out soups and stews (add 2 table-spoons of sautéed dried onions with each cup of liquid). They will add flavor to almost any bland vegetable; make an interesting topping for a casserole, combined with crushed potato chips or corn-flakes; or even make blah sandwiches unexpectedly good (how about dried onions, browned or not, with cheese or peanut butter or tuna fish?).

One box of grated Parmesan cheese. The ideal hurry-up topping. It hides a multitude of sins when used as a casserole topping and tastes good on most cooked vegetables, fish, and meats. Don't for-get a good sprinkling on a salad that needs something.

One box of instant vanilla pudding. A dessert's salvation. You can pad out skimpy pie fillings by using the pudding as a base layer, with the fruit on top. You can use it as a sauce over insufficient quantities of fruit or cake (see the recipe in Appendix F). You can even use it, we are told, to make vanilla pudding.

Two small cans or packages of hollandaise sauce. Who would ever dream you had made a mistake when you bring something to the table smothered in hollandaise? Use it straight on many vegetables, bland fish, or eggs. Add a pinch of tarragon and you have Béar-naise sauce for meat, fish, or vegetables. Add some tomato paste (2 tablespoons per can) and you have Choron sauce to pour on eggs or meat loaf. Warm it, add 1 tablespoon of grated orange peel and 2 tablespoons of orange juice per can and you have Maltaise sauce, which will make the most tasteless fish or vegetable something exotic.

One can of cheese sauce or cheese soup. Stir it into casseroles; pour it on vegetables. Heat it and pour on toast for instant Welsh rabbit. Use it to cover up a main dish that looks funny but tastes all right.

One big box of baking soda. You never want to be without it. Besides its cooking and medicinal uses, it is the ideal kitchen fire extinguisher—especially for grease fires. Simply pour lots on a fire.

Note: Trying to douse a grease fire with water will normally only make it worse.

One jar of meat tenderizer. Whenever you pay less than four dollars a pound for beef, it probably can't hurt to use tenderizer. And it works well on poultry and liver, too. Don't have qualms about the stuff—it is made from natural fruit enzymes (from papayas, actually), and it won't tenderize your insides.

One jar, bottle, or plastic lemon of reconstituted lemon juice. Lemon juice livens up older vegetables and doubtful fishes. Use it, too, whenever something is darkening that shouldn't: fruit slices, avocados, parsnips, etc. If you don't want the end product to have a lemony taste, rinse whatever-it-is under gently running cold water before going on. You can even make lemonade for unexpected company.

One box of prepared baking mix (like Bisquick). For fast-baked food, ranging from cookies and coffeecake to breads and biscuits, it is often terribly comforting to know that you are not more than 13 minutes away from homemade quick breads.

One box of mashed potato flakes. And not just so you can always have mashed potatoes. It is a fast and nutritious thickener for soups and stews. Just add by the handful until you've got the consistency you want. Also as a great extender for most vegetables you don't have enough of. Chop up the vegetable (for instance: carrots, beans, broccoli) after it is cooked and well drained. Combine with an equal amount of mashed potatoes. Top with Parmesan cheese, and run under the broiler 2 or 3 minutes, until the top is browned.

One large can of asparagus. To use whenever an extra vegetable is needed; to pad out an insufficient salad; or for the emergency meal of Appendix F.

One large can of pear halves. To use whenever an extra fruit is needed; to pad out an insufficient salad; or for the emergency meal of Appendix F.

Two jars of chipped beef. To keep on hand in case you ever need to make the emergency meal given in Appendix F. Chipped beef will last almost indefinitely. Make a note on your desk calendar to consider replacing it if you haven't used it in, say, eighty or ninety years.

One box of unflavored gelatin. For thickening cool things. Soften a package in ¼ cup of cold water, and add to 1 cup of warm liquid to dissolve it. Then add to aspic, pudding, pie filling, or whatever. It will even rescue a soggy croquette (see CROQUETTES). It is also a pretty good start for a lot of fancy desserts: check any good cookbook, or, better still, improvise!

One bottle of good sherry. Like hollandaise, sherry is a gourmet touch that turns disasters into "Oh-you-didn't-have-to-go-to-all-this-trouble" triumphs. It makes any stew, soup, or casserole taste richer. Start with 2 tablespoons in a 4- to 6-person potful, and keep tasting. You can sprinkle it lightly on a variety of desserts, from pudding to cake. And you can always serve it straight (or over ice) to your starving guests while you're busy patching things up. *One box of powdered milk.* So you'll never be without milk. Milk fanciers find powdered milk more acceptable when it has been refrigerated (after mixing it with water) for ½ hour. Use powdered milk anywhere you'd use whole milk: desserts, sauces, baths, etc. And you can make a whipped topping out of powdered milk, water, and lemon juice. See the dessert recipe in Appendix F.

One set of basic spices. A basic spice is one you can add to almost anything with some likelihood of improving and/or making more interesting the anything. Everyone has his own basics. Ours are the following:

CHILI POWDER and/or OREGANO (depending on whether you are more Mexican or Italian at heart)

CINNAMON (try it in entrées as well as in desserts and drinks)

CURRY POWDER

FINES HERBES

GARLIC SALT or POWDER (powder is stronger; salt is saltier)

PEPPER

The basic rule of thumb on herbs and spices is to add ¼ teaspoon for each pound of ingredients, and then start tasting. Use this amount throughout the suggestions in the book unless we advise you otherwise. Some foods will require much more than this; others (especially if you use cloves and saffron, for instance) may need less. Improvise and experiment with whatever you have on hand. And write down what you do, in case you come up with something great.

One set of assorted food colorings. Use them either to make things more the color you think they should be (a few drops of yellow in curried rice or bread dough; some red in the spaghetti sauce, etc.) or, for variety, to make things a color they shouldn't be (like pink mashed potatoes or blue lemonade).

15

You may ordinarily keep some of these things on hand. Buy the others, and tuck them away in an emergency corner of the cupboard. Sometimes true happiness is remembering you've got a box of dried onions stashed away.

Let us repeat, because we cannot say it often enough: *Improvise!* That is the key to success when something goes wrong. Think of it this way: What have you got to lose? As far as is known, there are no two foods which, when mixed together, will explode. The worst that can happen is that a partial disaster may be converted into a total disaster—perhaps even a glorious disaster, one your grandchildren will remember and discuss with awe.

And you may have surprising success. Look, if the Mexicans can pour chocolate sauce over poultry; if a well-known San Francisco restaurant can serve ice cream with pickles and hot fudge; if the Uruguayans can improve a fine steak by spreading peanut butter on it—*what have you got to lose?*

Improvise! Good luck.

at's carbonated, and whiskey, rum, brandy, and/or
r it up to taste (don't taste too much, please) with
, bitters, rosemary, nutmeg, and/or whole carda-

een or *after* meals, things are simpler. Make cap-
coffee, hot toddies, or brandied grog. Be sure you
ple what they want. Come in with the stuff all
they can't refuse.

and, missing something
at what's missing is something other than the al-
three seasonings that tend to give a punch punch:
om, nutmeg, and rosemary. For a punch bowl, dis-
teaspoon of rosemary, nutmeg, or powdered carda-
p of hot fruit juice, let it cool to room temperature,
the punch.

ce NUTS

the oil from the anchovy can to the salad dressing;
he salad taste considerably more anchovyful.
euvres, mash the anchovies up with cream cheese.
like spaghetti or pizza sauce), add the oil from the
ce before or during cooking.

Total Failure

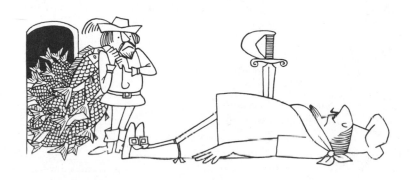

When you have a total, absolute, cannot-be-corrected, you've-tried-to-improvise-and-only-made-it-worse failure, there are three, and only three, paths open to you.

The first is to run yourself through with your sword. This may seem a bit extreme for a culinary bungle, but there is good historical precedent: the case of François Vatel, steward to the French Minister of Finance, who is still regarded as one of the Top Ten chefs of all time.

One day King Louis XIV came calling. Vatel prepared a great meal, but the king's party was larger than expected, and there wasn't enough food for everyone. Some had to make do with eggs or something.

Vatel was disconsolate, but he vowed to redeem himself the following day, which happened to be a Friday. Fresh fish was a rarity in those days, and Vatel had placed orders with fishermen all over France. Late that night he was called to the kitchen to accept delivery from one of the fishermen. He did not realize that this was only a small part of his order. "Is that all there is?" he asked in disbelief. "Yes," he was mistakenly told.

One failure was enough. Two in a row were literally unbearable. Vatel went up to his room and ran himself through with his sword. He was found dead a short time later when someone came to tell him that the rest of the fish had arrived.

Now, whatever you've done, it can't be that bad, can it? So please don't run yourself through with your sword. For that matter, don't even jab yourself with your shrimp deveiner. Try alternatives two or three.

The second alternative is to give up and let someone else do the cooking. In other words, find someone to take you out to dinner. (No, we don't know how to arrange that. This book solves *cooking* problems, not *social* problems.)

The third alternative is to whip up a gourmet meal in twenty minutes from a simple set of ingredients you've already got on hand. This is entirely possible, but only if you have all the emergency ingredients described a few pages back. If you believed us when we suggested you keep a kitchen "first-aid kit" on hand, turn now to Appendix F, and you will find a pretty good dinner for four that can be made from scratch in about twenty minutes.

Don't forget to replace any emergency ingredients you may use. We don't want to sound too pessimistic, but, as Mrs. Vatel may have said to her husband on Thursday night, "Who knows what may happen tomorrow?"

Alp

ABALONE: see FISH

ALCOHOL: see also
For *major* problems
telephone book for y
problems:

Brandy or liqueur w
It's probably not h
worry if it isn't),
about the extra bran
your guests shouldn
dish.) Heat it slowly
ignite in the pan.
away.) When hot,
the *liquid*. Say, may

Drink tastes too alc
We don't know e
mainly middle-aged
floating a thin slice
slices of cucumber
tasting.

Not enough
If you're stuck wit
dinner, try making

you've got th
vodka. Doct
sugar, lemon
mom.

If it's *betu*
puccino, Iris
don't ask pe
mixed up an

Punch too b
Assuming th
cohol, here a
whole cardan
solve about 1
mom in ½ cu
and add it to

ALMONDS:

ANCHOVIES
Not enough
In salads, ad
it will make
In hors d'c
In sauces (
can to the sa

Salty
Soak the anchovies in clear tap water for about 10 minutes. Pat them dry with paper towels. If you don't intend to use them right away, store in a container with enough olive oil to cover them. (No olive oil? All right, some other kind of cooking oil.)

APPLES, COOKED: see also APPLES, RAW
Bland
Sprinkle on some powdered ginger, mace, coriander, and/or add a clove bag to the apples. Or dump some caraway seeds (mixed with sugar), some fennel, or some grated lemon or orange peel down the hole of a blah baked apple and cook it 10 minutes more.

Burned
See Appendix A: BURNED FOODS.

Not enough
If the apples are going to be served with meat, augment them with quartered onions sautéed until soft (about 10 minutes) in 1 tablespoon per medium-sized onion of butter, in a covered saucepan. Add a handful of raisins (optional) that you have plumped in a cup of boiling water and drained.

If the apples are for dessert, combine with cranberries or any other kind of berries or pitted cherries or canned pineapple, or add fresh sliced pears when the apples are about half-cooked, plus 1 teaspoon of vanilla extract and an extra ⅛ teaspoon of cinnamon. (If you use winter pears, you may have to add more sugar.) You can add canned apricots if you're desperate, but be sure to drain them well, pit them, and then rename your dessert. The apricots will now be the dominant taste.

APPLES, RAW: see also APPLES, COOKED
Bland
Dip diced or quartered apples, peeled or un, in powdered anise. Or sprinkle on some powdered cinnamon, nutmeg, and/or poppy

seed. In fruit salad, try mashed-up rosemary or powdered cardamom. (Stir ¼ teaspoon of either into ½ cup of honey, and spoon it over sliced apples.) Improvise!

Discoloring
Apples do this when their flesh is exposed to the air. Rub a little lemon juice on the exposed flesh. If it is already unpleasantly dark, cut off the dark layer. No lemon juice? Dunk the apple pieces in slightly salted water until you're ready for them. Or, if the taste is compatible, submerge them in pineapple juice instead.

Mealy
There is no way known to unmeal an apple. No matter what you were *planning* to do, make applesauce.

ARTICHOKE HEARTS: see also ARTICHOKES

Frozen to box
Run cold water into the box, and after a few seconds the artichokes should dislodge themselves.

Pickledy
Artichoke-heart lovers will know what that means; for the rest of you, it doesn't matter. Soak the hearts in clear water for 10 minutes, and then, if you aren't going to use them at once, store covered with olive (or, if you have none, some other kind of cooking) oil. Guaranteed less pickledy.

Thawed
If frozen artichoke hearts have thawed and you didn't want them to, see Appendix B.

ARTICHOKES

Bland
The best thing is a tiny, tiny, wee bit of fennel (about ⅛ teaspoon) in the cooking water. Once they are fully cooked, you'll have to add flavoring to the butter you dip the leaves in; for instance, a shake of Tabasco sauce in the butter. Or use hol-

landaise sauce instead of butter. Or make Instant Phony Béarnaise sauce by adding a good pinch of tarragon to the hollandaise. Or use vinaigrette (3 parts oil to 1 part vinegar) on either hot or cold artichokes.

Burned

The only way to burn an artichoke is to boil away all the water. This time cut away the burned part, see Appendix H for burned pots, and resume cooking.

Next time use more water. A big potful can't possibly boil away—at least not before the artichoke is dreadfully overcooked. Steamed artichoke people: Be careful!

Hard to drain

Put something absorbent, like a washcloth or lots of paper towels, in the bottom of a bowl. Turn the artichoke upside down in the bowl. (Please clean the washcloth before using it on yourself. If artichoke balm were any good for us, you can be sure the cosmetic people would be selling it to us on the television.)

Old

If your artichokes have been around awhile, add a pinch of sugar and ¼ teaspoon of salt to each cup of water you use to cook them in. The sugar sweetens them just a tiny bit (what else?), and the salt helps retain color and flavor.

If your old artichokes *look* funny, try removing the outer leaves—they may still be lovely inside.

Separating, falling apart

Once it has started, there isn't much you can do. A good way to keep it from happening next time is to wrap the artichokes in cheesecloth before cooking, and remove the cheesecloth just before serving.

ASPARAGUS

Bland

Add bouillon to the cooking water. Sprinkle the asparagus with ground mustard seed or ground sesame seed. Or use seasoned salt. Or flavored butter. Or Japanese soy sauce.

Frozen to box
Run a bit of cold tap water into the spaces in the carton; the asparagus should loosen up at once.

Not enough
Extend meager asparagus supplies by making:

Aunt Helene's Scalloped Asparagus

Heat the oven to 375°. Open 2 cans of white sauce—or, if you're a purist, *make* 2 cups of white sauce (medium)—and add 1 teaspoon of Worcestershire, ¼ teaspoon of pepper, ⅓ cup of any kind of cheese you have on hand (like Parmesan or Cheddar or Velveeta), or a whole jar of pimento cheese spread, or, if you have no cheese at all, 3 tablespoons of sherry, or, if you have no sherry (you can't say we're not trying), 1 tablespoon of onion powder or 2 tablespoons of fresh grated onion. Drain the asparagus and put it in a baking dish. Shred a piece of toast over it. Pour the sauce over that. Sprinkle paprika on the sauce, and bake for 15 minutes.

Old
Add a pinch of sugar (for sweetness) and ¼ teaspoon of salt (to help retain color and flavor) to each cup of cooking water.

Overcooked
If you haven't any time to spare, you'll have to serve mushy asparagus. If you have an hour or so, here is one of the world's great recipes utilizing overcooked asparagus:

Timbale d'Asperges

Sauté ½ cup minced onions for 5 minutes. Put them in a big bowl. Add ¼ teaspoon salt, a pinch of nutmeg, a big pinch of white pepper, ½ cup grated cheese (preferably Swiss; any will do), ⅓ cup bread crumbs (preferably stale). Beat in 2 eggs. Bring 1 cup milk to a boil and beat into the mix. Mash the

24

overcooked asparagus into the mix (anywhere from 1 to 2 cups). Grease a 2-quart mold or baking pan. Coat the mold or pan with ¼ cup bread crumbs. Turn the mix into the mold or pan. Bake at the bottom of your oven for 35 to 40 minutes, having set the mold in a pan of very hot water. Adjust the oven heat so that the water is just simmering—roughly 275°. It is done when a knife in the center comes out clean. Serve on a warm platter, either plain or with an interesting sauce, like *sauce mousseline*.

Sauce Mousseline
Chill ½ cup whipped cream; fold into 1½ cups hollandaise sauce.

If you're short of time, but you've got a can of cream of anything soup on hand, blend the overcooked asparagus to a mush, combine with the soup, and serve hot as a first course.

Salty
Once they're on your plate and you've salted them too much, you can put asparagus spears back in plain hot water for 1 minute. Add a dash of any sort of vinegar to the water.
If you've oversalted the cooking water, change it at once.

Thawed
See Appendix B regarding frozen food that has thawed before you're ready for it.

Too much
Cook it all, refrigerate. Next day make recipe on page 26.

Oriental Salad Paddington

Cut up the chilled asparagus (you did refrigerate it, didn't you?), and combine with lettuce, pimentos (or sweet red peppers or tomatoes if you absolutely have to), and chopped green onions. Dress with a mixture of 1 part lemon juice to 2 parts salad oil and a dash of salt. (Use a dash of soy sauce instead of salt, if you have any.) Cover with ¼ cup sesame seeds that have been toasted in a 350° oven on a cooky sheet for 5 minutes, and serve.

ASPIC: see GELATIN

AVOCADOS

Darkening
The simplest method to inhibit darkening is to restore the avocado meat to the vicinity of the pit. The pit somehow, perhaps magically, retards darkness. If you've only cut the avocado in half, close it back up around the pit. If the meat is in a bowl, put the pit in the bowl.

A less magical but just as effective method is to sprinkle lemon or lime juice on the exposed flesh.

Hard to peel
There is no easy way to peel an avocado. But many avocados are peeled unnecessarily. There is often no need. Do this instead: Cut it in half lengthwise, and separate the two halves. Wham the blade (not the point) of a big knife into the pit, twist it, and the pit will come neatly out. Now you can scoop the meat out with a spoon or, for variety in salads, with a melon baller.

Not enough
In a salad, avocado combines well with citrus fruit sections. In a tossed salad, don't worry; no one will notice.

In a dip, fill it out with cream cheese softened with milk to avocado consistency. When mixed in well and seasoned again, it will never show. If you're still worried, add a drop of green food coloring.

Too many
Whole avocados should be stored in the refrigerator; they won't ripen (or overripen) as fast. To preserve the appearance and increase the longevity of sliced avocados, coat the exposed parts with butter or margarine. Then you can keep them for days in the refrigerator. Smear the fat on thick for best results.

Uncertain quality
Press the avocado with your thumb. If it dents easily, it is ready to use. If the grocer complains, tell him we said it was all right.

Unripe
Seal the avocado in a brown paper bag, and keep it in a warm but not hot place. If the avocado has already been cut open and found to be unripe, coat the exposed surfaces with margarine or butter and do likewise.

BACON

Curling
Once it is fairly curly, the only thing to do is to put something heavy and flat on it (like a pot full of water), right on the griddle. Or, if it is already cooked and hopelessly curly, why not break it into small pieces and drop it into the eggs or whatever?

If it is just beginning to curl, dust the top lightly with flour, and the curling should be retarded.

Next time *bake* the bacon at 400° for 10 to 15 minutes instead of grilling or broiling it. Baked bacon tastes just the same, but it lies there flat as a pancake.

On fire
Small fire: drop a pot or pan on top of it to snuff it out. Big fire: pour on baking soda or salt. Lots.

Stuck together
Method 1: roll the entire package up crosswise. Unroll, and unless the pigs were fed on a diet of glue, all the bacon strips should be unstuck.

Method 2: Drop the whole stuck-together bundle onto the griddle, under the broiler, or in the oven, and it will come unstuck as it cooks.

BAKED BEANS: see BEANS, BAKED

BAKING POWDER

Have none, need some
For every cup of flour in the recipe, mix 2 teaspoons of cream of tartar, 1 teaspoon of bicarbonate of soda, and ½ teaspoon of salt. Use this right away; it won't be effective for more than a day or so.

If your recipe happens to use buttermilk or sour milk, you can add ¼ teaspoon of baking soda to each ½ cup of milk in the recipe.

Uncertain quality
Stale baking powder can ruin whatever you're making. But old powder isn't necessarily stale. Here is a test for baking powder staleness: Put 1 teaspoonful in a cup of hot water. If it bubbles a lot, it's good. If it doesn't, throw it out.

BANANAS

Bland
Sprinkle sliced bananas with anise, cinnamon, or nutmeg, for example.

Darkening

Coat the banana slices with lemon juice. If they are already dark, slice each slice in half, and arrange them good side up; no one will know the difference. Some old wives claim that bananas sliced with a silver knife don't darken as quickly.

Not enough

You'll have to fill out with something. Ripe pears go well with bananas without imposing too much on the flavor or smoothness. In a salad, try a cantaloupe to keep a lonely banana company; the colors are lovely together, and the taste isn't bad, either.

Overripe, mushy

Here are two very simple and good things made from overripe or mushy bananas:

Banana Eggnog à la Mariah

Blend together 1 mushy banana, 1 cup of cold milk, 1 egg, and a dash of salt. Drink.

Susannah's Roast Bananas

Remove one thin strip of peel. Brush the exposed banana meat with butter. Roast in the oven (400°) or over coals until the entire peel is black. Eat directly from the peel with a spoon.

Too many (and they're all ripe at once)

Well, you'll just have to make a banana cream pie. This can

be absurdly simple if you use a store-bought pie shell, canned vanilla pudding, and spray-on whipped cream topping. See your favorite cookbook for details.

What—you still have more? All right, mash them up, combine with lemon juice (1 lemon for each 6 bananas; or you can use that citric-acid stuff groceries sell for home fruit processing), and freeze in an airtight container or in freezer wrap. See, Chiquita, you *can* put bananas in the refrigerator! Now you have six months to find some interesting recipes for mashed bananas. Like banana bread, banana cake, and banana pudding, for starters. Thaw fully before unwrapping or opening, or the banana will turn brown. Even if it does, the taste is unimpaired.

BEAN SOUP: see soups

BEANS, BAKED

Bland
Stir in some catchup or chili sauce or Tabasco sauce or brown sugar or rosemary or (what the heck) all of them.

Burned
See Appendix A, regarding burned foods.

Not enough
Combine them with Lima beans or kidney beans. Add brown sugar, or molasses and sugar, or maple syrup to make them taste more beany.

Salty
If they're very salty, about all you can do is add more beans. But not more salt, for goodness sake. If just slightly salty, a little brown sugar and/or a little vinegar will tend to override the salty flavor.

Time is short
Beans for baking should soak overnight. If you don't have time to do that, do this: Add 1 teaspoon of baking powder to 1

pound or so of beans, cover them with water, and cook at medium heat until they are soft but not mushy—about 40 minutes. Add more water if necessary while they cook. Then drain off the water, and bake as usual.

Uncertain quality
Dump the raw beans in water. The good ones will sink, and the bad ones will float. Just as in real life.

BEANS, LIMA AND STRING

The two kinds are combined because most of the problems facing the bean world are shared by the two of them.

Bland
A pinch of sugar in the cooking water helps bring out the flavor. On the plate or in the pot, try adding dillseed, fennel, or rosemary. Sage perks up Lima beans (⅛ teaspoon in the cooking water), and sesame seed, sprinkled on string beans, is interesting.

Frozen to box
Run cold water into the spaces in the box, and the beans will shortly come out.

Losing color
When beans start losing color, and when it is *very important* to you that they don't, then you may add a pinch of baking soda to the water. It will help them retain their color, but it will also extract most of the vitamins.

Not enough
In every San Francisco Italian restaurant, of which there are at least 73,000 excellent ones, you find something called Italian vegetables. Usually, but not always, they are a mixture of Italian beans, peas, and string beans. Very good. If you're desperate, even kidney or navy beans or chopped broccoli will do. Add a sizable chunk of butter, and cook together for 5 minutes so the flavors blend.

Old
If your string beans or Lima beans have been around for a week or more, add a pinch of sugar and ¼ teaspoon of salt to the cooking water.

Stringy
If your Lima beans are stringy, you have more problems than this book can help you with. For stringy string beans, plunge them into boiling water for 3 minutes. Drain the water. The strings should virtually fall off.

Thawed
See Appendix B for a comment and a suggestion.

Too many
Lima beans reheat beautifully, especially if you brown ½ cup of minced onions and add them to the pot with a few tablespoons of water when reheating. Crumbled bacon on top is a nice touch. Just don't worry about Lima beans.

String beans make excellent salad material when cold. Before putting them in the refrigerator, dress them with a mixture of 3 parts oil to 1 part lemon juice or vinegar. Salt and pepper to taste, and if you've got some dill, add a couple of pinches. No dill? How about a dill pickle? Chop it fine, and add it to the beans. Remember that the pickle will add salt, so be careful in that department.

BEEF: see specific kinds of beef in the following categories:
BOILED BEEF, CHIPPED BEEF, CORNED BEEF, HAMBURGERS, LIVER, MEAT LOAF, POT ROAST, ROAST BEEF, STEAK, and STEW

BEET GREENS: see GREENS

BEETS
Bland
Add a pinch of ground cloves or allspice to the cooking water. Or chervil (about ¼ teaspoon per serving). Or sprinkle the

cooked beets with dill weed or mustard seed. Experiment with other seasonings. Beets are very adaptable.

Discoloring
Add 1 tablespoon of lemon juice or vinegar to the cooking water. Next time do this at the start, just in case; it can do no harm.

Frozen to box
Run some cold tap water into the carton, and the beets should unstick themselves forthwith.

Hard to peel
Beets virtually peel themselves if you treat them right. Just like—well, never mind. Put them in water, leaving about ½ inch of stem and root on them. Boil for 15 minutes. Then put them under cold running water. Cut off both ends, and the peel should slip right off.

Not enough
Beets and greens are a good combination. Cook the beet greens separately, and mix with cooked, diced beets. (Spinach, mustard, or other greens will do as well; in a pinch, so will lettuce leaves.) Add 1 tablespoon of vinegar and 1 teaspoon of sugar. If you are a bacon-fat saver, now's your chance. Add a scant tablespoon to the cooking water for a Southern flavor.

33

Old
Add a pinch of sugar and a pinch of salt for each cup of liquid you're cooking the beets in. The former sweetens them back to their natural sweetness; the latter helps retain color and flavor.

Salty
If pickled beets are too salty, soak them in clear water for 10 minutes, and restore them in new water.

If cooked beets are too salty, add a dash of either sugar or vinegar—or both—to the cooking water.

Too many
Of course you can always pickle them (see how under BEANS, LIMA AND STRING, *Too many*, and omit the dill). Or, better yet, surprise everyone tomorrow with this easy borsch:

Aunt Esther's Borsch
Cook 1 pound cut-up beef-stew-type beef for 1½ to 2 hours, or until the beef is tender, in a package of dehydrated vegetable soup, using twice the amount of water called for on the package. Add leftover beets and either 2 teaspoons dill weed or ½ teaspoon fresh dill or 1 teaspoon dillseed, and cook 10 minutes more. Serve with sour cream on top. A boiled potato in each bowl makes this a whole meal.

BERRIES
Bland
Sprinkle with brown sugar, confectioners' sugar, or one of the slightly sweet seasonings, like nutmeg, cinnamon, or anise seed. If there is some juice, drop a whole cardamon or two into it during storage.

Frozen to box
Run cold tap water into the box, and the berries will detach themselves almost at once.

Leafy, twiggy
Sometimes there are lots of little leaves and twigs mixed in

with the berries, especially if you've picked them yourself. The fastest way to deleaf and detwig a large pail of berries is to pour them from one container to another across the path of an electric fan or a vacuum cleaner hose fastened to the blowing instead of the sucking nozzle. Please aim the air in the right direction; otherwise see a good first-aid text on removing berry twigs from the ear.

Not enough
In a pie, use your emergency vanilla pudding and make it a berry cream pie. Either use the berries and the pudding in layers, or mix them together. Top with a meringue, and everyone will think that was what you meant all along.

With a shortcake, combine berries with fresh peaches, nectarines, or even pears. If you use pears, mix them with a sauce made from ¼ cup of water, 2 tablespoons of sugar, and ¼ teaspoon of almond extract, to give them more flavor.

Overripe
Make fruit sauce. Clean the berries as well as you can, eliminating all fuzzy ones. Mash the rest with the sugar to taste (start with about 1 tablespoon per cup), and serve with ice cream or shortcake or cream.

Or use them in a deep-dish pie or a cobbler. Overripe berries are very juicy, but this won't matter if you have only a top crust.

Sour
Stir them with sugar and allow to stand at room temperature for at least an hour. Use about 1 tablespoon per cup of berries.

Thawed
See Appendix B, regarding frozen foods that have thawed out too soon.

Too many
Clean and spread them out one layer deep on a cooky sheet. Freeze until firm, and pour them into some sort of storage

35

container; freezer bags do nicely. Then, when berries are out of season, you will have the equivalent of fresh ones and not the sugar-soaked kind you usually have to settle for.

Another alternative is to make jelly or jam. Consult any good cookbook for instructions; it isn't nearly as hard as you probably think it is.

Wet

Nobody likes a wet berry. Line a big tray or cooky sheet with paper towels. Pour the berries on it. Pat them with more paper towels on top. Gently.

BISCUITS: see BREAD, ROLLS, MUFFINS

BLACKBERRIES: see BERRIES

BLUEBERRIES: see BERRIES

BOILED BEEF: see CORNED BEEF

BOUILLON: see SOUPS

BOYSENBERRIES: see BERRIES

BRANDY: see ALCOHOL

BREAD, ROLLS, MUFFINS: see also CAKE; COOKIES; PIES

Bland

Once it's made, you can't make the *bread* more interesting, so put interesting things *on* it. For the breadbasket at dinner, try making interesting-flavored butters. Cream butter with herbs, spices, grated onion, crushed garlic. For instance, try adding ½ teaspoon ground thyme, marjoram, or crushed basil to ½ stick of butter. Or add a few drops of lemon juice for lemon butter. Or grind up a bit of whatever the main course is (meat or fish, for instance) and mash it up with the butter.

Next time sprinkle on anise or toasted poppy seed or sesame seed before baking. Or sift some sage (1 tablespoon per loaf) or poultry seasoning in with the flour. If the main course is ham or pork, try ¼ teaspoon cinnamon and 1 teaspoon sugar in the bread dough.

Burned
If you are baking or heating bread and it burns slightly, you can remove the burned spots with an ordinary kitchen grater. This is not recommended with burned toast.

If there are lots of burned spots, you can cut them off and patch up the scars with bread ointment. Bread ointment is simply a well-beaten egg. Brush it on the wounds with a pastry brush, and keep on heating the bread.

Cold
There are two ways to make cold bread hot without cooking it any more. For crusty kinds of bread and rolls, dip them very briefly in a bowl of hot water, and toss them in a 350° oven until they are as hot as you'd like. For softer breads and muffins, wrap them rather loosely in foil and heat for 5 minutes at 450°.

Dried out
Wrap the bread or rolls in a damp towel and refrigerate for 24 hours. Then remove the towel and heat the bread in the oven at 350° for 5 minutes. It should be restored to something close to its normal condition.

Hard to slice
Heat the knife.

To slice soft bread very thin, about the only thing to do is freeze it, slice it, and defrost it.

Soggy
If sandwiches are needed and the bread is soggy, go ahead and make sandwiches anyway; then grill the whole works briefly under the broiler. Unless you're given to making ice cream sandwiches, it shouldn't hurt the ingredients.

Stale
Here are two fast techniques that often help revitalize stale bread:

1. Pour ½ teaspoon of water on the bread, seal it up in a brown paper bag, and heat it in a 350° oven for 10 to 15 minutes.

2. Plunge the entire loaf (or rolls or whatever) into cold water for just an instant; then bake on a tin at 350° for 10 minutes.

Small amounts of very stale bread can, of course, be used to make bread crumbs. If a whole loaf should go stale on you, here is an interesting Italian recipe to use it up:

Mozzarella Roberto Bomani

With the same cooky cutter, cut out 20 slices (or so) of stale bread and 10 slices (or so) of thick mozzarella cheese (up to ¼ inch thick). Make 10 (or so) sandwiches. Dip the edges of the bread into a mixture of ½ cup milk and ½ cup bread crumbs. Dip the whole thing in 2 eggs beaten up with ½ teaspoon salt. Fry in 1 cup olive oil or butter and serve.

Stuck to muffin tin
Put the muffin tin on a wet towel. In a couple of minutes, the muffins should come free.

Stuck to pan
If bread sticks to whatever you're cooking or heating it in, wrap the whole works (bread and pan) in a dry towel while it is hot, and let it cool outside the oven for 5 minutes. Unwrap and presto!

Stuck to rolling pin
If bread dough sticks to the rolling pin and you don't want to add more flour by flouring the rolling pin, put the rolling pin in the freezer until it is very cold, and then roll out the dough.

Won't rise

When bread dough fails to rise, additional gentle heat often helps. If you have an electric heating pad, set it on low, put foil on the pad, and put the bowl of dough on the foil.

Another way to produce gentle heat is to put the bowl in the dishwasher and set for just the drying cycle. (If you make a mistake here, see BREAD, ROLLS, MUFFINS, *Soggy*.)

Or put the bowl in your gas oven; the warmth from the pilot light may be enough. Or put it in any oven over a large pan of boiling-hot water. A broiler-panful will do nicely.

BROCCOLI

Bland

Mustard seed does interesting things to broccoli: either in the cooking water or sprinkled lightly over the finished product.

Frozen to box

Run cold tap water into the box. The broccoli will come up for air promptly.

Not enough

Cover it up with hollandaise sauce. Everyone knows hollandaise sauce is *terribly* rich, so they'll eat less.

Or mash it up and combine with cream of chicken soup or pea soup. Sprinkle with Parmesan cheese, paprika, and croutons, and you've got either a soup course or an interesting side dish.

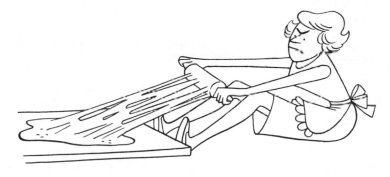

Old

When you cook old broccoli, add a pinch of sugar and a pinch of salt to each cup of cooking water.

Overcooked

If you have an awful lot of mushy broccoli, see the recipe for overcooked asparagus in the ASPARAGUS section, and try that, substituting broccoli for the asparagus. You may then prefer to call the dish Timbale de Broccoli. Or you may call it anything you like. There are those of us who think that naming dishes can be one of the more enjoyable things about cooking.

Salty

If you've put too much salt in the cooking pot, first change the water; then rinse off the broccoli gently under hot water, holding it in a sieve or colander; and return it to the pot.

If broccoli on the plate is oversalted, wash it off the same way in very hot water. Kitchen Bouquet has the tendency to overcome slight oversaltiness in broccoli.

Smelly

Is cooking broccoli smelling up the house? The neighborhood? Chuck a piece of bread or, better still, a small piece of red pepper into the pot.

Thawed

Please turn to Appendix B for one man's opinion of what to do when frozen food is prematurely thawed out.

Too much

Cooked broccoli will keep well for five days or so in the refrigerator. So, as soon as you're ready, you can make:

Broccoli à la Bonnie

Mix 3 eggs, ½ cup milk, 1½ cups grated Cheddar cheese, a dash of nutmeg, and a pinch of pepper. Lay the broccoli in a baking dish (the quantity is not important), pour the mixture over it, and bake in a 350° oven for 30 minutes. Since what you are really doing is making a sort of broccoli custard, it is wise to rest the baking dish inside a larger one with about an inch of water on the bottom.

BROTH: see soups

BROWN SUGAR: see sugar

BROWNIES: see cake

BRUSSELS SPROUTS

Everything said about broccoli, with the exception of *Overcooked,* applies equally well to Brussels sprouts. Please do not try to make Timbale de Brussels Sprouts.

Overcooked

Like building a perpetual-motion machine and trisecting the angle, devising a recipe for overcooked Brussels sprouts had long been thought to be impossible. We have cracked the Brussels sprouts barrier!

Brussels Sprouts Yeng Ling

Drain the overcooked little devils as gently and thoroughly as possible. Meanwhile, combine 1 tablespoon of oil, 2 tablespoons of vinegar, 1 tablespoon of sugar (preferably brown), and ½ teaspoon of soy sauce (or ¼ teaspoon of salt) in a saucepan, and bring to a boil. Now put a layer of soft crumbs in a baking dish, about ½ inch thick (the crumbs, not the dish). Lay the sprouts on the crumbs. Pour the sauce on them, and cover with a flurry of more crumbs and a little grated Parmesan cheese if you like it. You can keep this warm in the oven at 250°, but since it's already overcooked, don't wait too long.

BUTTER AND MARGARINE

Burning (while sautéing or frying food)

Add a tiny bit of any kind of oil (except motor oil) to the butter when you see it is browning too fast. It doesn't change the flavor, and oil plus butter doesn't burn as easily as butter alone. Badly burned butter does have a distinctive taste, so if you have enough extra butter, why not start over? If you don't, pour off the unburned butter, mix with oil, and a little butter flavoring if you have it, and hope for the best.

Have none, need some
In baking, an acceptable substitute for 1 cup of butter is 1 cup plus 2 tablespoons of Crisco. If a buttery flavor is required, add a few drops of butter flavoring. Of course, *no* one has butter flavoring on hand, so when you send your husband out to get some, ask him to pick up a pound or two of butter. . . .

For purposes other than baking, see the suggestion under WHIPPED CREAM, *Overwhipped, separated.*

Too hard to cream
Either shred the butter with a grater or potato peeler into a warmed bowl, or, if you're using sugar, try heating it slightly before adding it.

Too hard to spread
The problem is to soften the butter without melting it. The solution is to cover the butter with a hot bowl for a few minutes.

CABBAGE
Bland
Try adding any or all of the following three seeds to the cooking water: dill, mustard, and sesame.

Discoloring

Red cabbage sometimes turns purple or blue while cooking. Add 1 tablespoon of vinegar to the cooking water and it will turn red again.

Not enough

Cold cabbage (slaws and salads) fills out well with lettuce, shredded carrots, and diced celery and combines beautifully with pineapple (top with chopped nuts), apples (dice with the peel on, and add 1 tablespoon of horseradish to the dressing), and pears (add 1 teaspoon of curry powder for each cup of pears to the dressing, and top with a small mound of plumped raisins).

Hot cabbage can be sliced up into smaller pieces (assuming it was in wedges) and put into a baking dish. This is a messy job, but don't worry; it will come out looking all right. Pour cheese sauce or melted cheese over it all. Run under the broiler until it just begins to brown. Have any bacon crumbles? Thought not; all right, decorate with nuts (like toasted almonds), sliced olives, or good old paprika. Perhaps a shake or two of caraway seeds.

If you have tomatoes on hand, you might consider making:

Cabbage Ranchero

Fry some onions (dehydrated ones are fine) in butter. Chop some tomatoes, and add to the onions. (The quantities are tremendously variable; how far do you want to stretch the fool cabbage, anyway?) Cook 10 minutes, stirring occasionally. Toss in the cooked cabbage, which you have chopped up a bit. Add a couple of tablespoons of catchup and a couple of pinches of chili powder, and there you are.

Old

Add a pinch of salt to each cup of cooking water. This will help elderly cabbage retain during cooking what flavor it has left.

Overcooked

Make cabbage soup (see CABBAGE, *Too much*, for directions).

43

Or drain the cabbage *very well* by patting in paper towels after draining in colander. If it survives this treatment, it is probably edible as is. Toss it with butter in a warmed bowl, and season with garlic salt and pepper.

Smelly
The old-wives' remedy to prevent cabbage from stinking up the entire block is to put a piece of bread in the pot along with the cabbage. Rye bread seems to work the best, but any sort will have some effect in this antipollution campaign.

If the cabbage smell is already everywhere in the house, there is a good way to overcome it, if you like the smell of cloves. The odor of cloves tends to blot out the odor of cabbage. Produce eau de clove by simmering 3 or 4 whole cloves in a pan with a cup of vinegar in it. If you should decide the cloves smell worse than the cabbage, you're out of luck.

Too much
For raw cabbage, wrap well in plastic wrap or aluminum foil. It will keep a week if it is fresh. Worry about it next Thursday.

For cooked cabbage, chop it up and refrigerate it. Tomorrow you get:

Camilla's Cabbage-Chicken Potage
Combine cooked cabbage with a can of cream of chicken soup diluted with milk. Toast and butter a slice of rye bread (preferably with seeds) for each serving. (If you don't have rye bread, put a teaspoon of caraway seeds into the soup.) Put it in a bowl. Pour hot soup over the bread, and let it stand 3 minutes to sog the rye. This is good topped with shredded cheese and/or toasted almonds.

CAKE: see also BREAD, ROLLS, MUFFINS; COOKIES; CREAM PUFFS; ICING

Bubbles in the batter
Put the batter in the pan. Hold the pan about 6 inches above

44

the floor. Drop it. Do this 3 or 4 times or until the man from downstairs comes up to complain, whichever occurs first. The bubbles will go away. Perhaps the man from downstairs will, too.

Burned
If the cake is fully cooked, either cut away the burned parts and cover the cake with icing (even if you hadn't intended to), or use a steel grater to scrape away burned spots.

If the cake is not cooked fully but the top is too brown, cut away the burned parts and cover the wounds with a first-aid dressing made from a beaten egg mixed with 1 teaspoon of brown sugar. Brush it on with a pastry brush, and continue baking.

Crumbly; can't ice or slice
Freeze it; ice it; slice it; thaw it. Sis-boom-bah.

Drying out
If you intend to use the cake fairly soon, brush some melted butter on the top and sides. This retards drying and also makes it easier to spread the icing on.

If the cake is drying out in storage, put something moist in with the cake underneath the cake cover, which should be as airtight as possible. The most moist thing of all is a small glass of water. A slice of apple or orange will do nicely, too. Don't forget to add water or change slices every 2 or 3 days.

Remember, too, that most cakes can successfully be frozen.

Flat, soggy, fallen

If your cake is flat or soggy, you probably forgot to put in the baking powder. No known remedial measures can correct this condition. As Escoffier (or maybe it was Joe at the Greasy Spoon) said, "The cake shall never rise again."

But fallen cake still *tastes* pretty good, even if it looks awful. Use your imagination to come up with an interesting fallen-cake recipe. One example should suffice:

Tanya's Apple Moosh

Break fallen cake into chunks. Mix with sweetened canned applesauce, and serve with whipped cream. No one will ever know it wasn't intentional.

Lopsided

Check your cake after 20 minutes of cooking, as a rule. If it is going to turn out lopsided because of a listing kitchen or a defective oven or whatever, turn it (the cake) around halfway. Check again after another 20 minutes. Keep turning if necessary.

Stale

Unfortunately, there is no good way to unstale a cake. Fortunately, there are a lot of dessert recipes that work very well, sometimes even better, with stale cake. Check your big cookbooks. We suggest these two things to do with stale cake—one chocolate and one vanilla:

Cousin Gail's Chocolate Meringue Treat

Cut stale chocolate cake in cubes. Pile on thickly a meringue made from 6 teaspoons of sugar to 1 egg white. Sprinkle with grated coconut or chopped pecans. Heat in a 300° oven until the meringue is brown.

Vanilla Rum Delight à la Charles

Cut stale cake in cubes. Sprinkle 1 tablespoon of rum for each cup of cake. Mix into thick vanilla pudding. Chill. Serve with whipped cream.

Stuck to cellophane wrapper

Iced packaged cakes tend to stick to their wrappers. Hold the package under the cold-water faucet for about 20 to 30 seconds before unwrapping. This works better if the water is turned on.

Stuck to pan

This is one of the most fertile areas for household-hint thinker-uppers. Many techniques have been proposed, and they all have merit:

1. Let the cake sit for 5 minutes; it will shrink a little and may be easier to remove.

2. Remove the pan from the oven, and place it on a cloth which you have soaked in cold water and wrung out.

3. Loosen the edges with a knitting needle rather than a knife, place a wire rack on top, invert the whole works, and tap the bottom of the pan, if necessary, with a spoon.

4. Wrap the cake and pan in a towel as it comes from the oven, and let it stand for 5 minutes.

5. If the cake is cold and stuck, reheat it for a few minutes.

Stuck to rolling pin

What are you doing rolling out cake dough? Ah, well, if you must, chill the rolling pin in the freezer, and the dough won't stick.

Too soft; can't ice or slice

Freeze it; ice it; slice it; thaw it. Rah, team, rah.

CANDY

Fudge (and other such) too hard

Before cooking: If the fudge won't pour, add 1 tablespoon of milk and 2 or 3 tablespoons of corn syrup; beat until smooth; pour at once.

During cooking: Add a little milk and cook to the proper temperature.

After cooking: Put in an airtight container. The fudge should become softer and more velvety in 24 hours.

Fudge won't fudge
Fudge that won't fudge (fudge makers will know what this means) is almost certainly not cooked enough. Scrape it back into the saucepan, add a teaspoon or two of water, and keep cooking, stirring constantly.

Stuck together
If hard candies stick together in the jar or bowl, separate them by hand (unless you have a machine for the purpose), and sprinkle loosely with granulated (or, better yet, superfine granulated) sugar before returning them to the container.

Sugaring
When chocolate candies start sugaring while cooking, add a little bit of milk, and keep cooking until they return to the prescribed temperature.

CANS
Key is missing
Try using a regular can opener on the opposite side. Write a nasty letter to the manufacturer.

Key is stuck halfway through opening can
Holding the can with a dishtowel or oven mitt, try sticking a table knife through the hole in the key handle to get more leverage. (If you use your bare hands, get the Band-Aids out first.) If this fails and the contents can't be scraped out, hold the can over a bowl and try a can opener on the other side. Write a *very* nasty letter to the manufacturer.

CARROTS
Bland
Try adding any of the following seasonings to cooked carrots:

roughly ¼ teaspoon per 4 servings of bay leaf, ground cloves, ginger, mace, marjoram, poppy seed, sesame, or thyme. Consider catchup or chili sauce over cooked carrots.

Burned
See Appendix A regarding burned foods.

Frozen to box
Run cold water into the carton to unstick frozen carrots.

Not enough
For raw carrots, use with any other raw vegetable on a relish plate; or shave them with a vegetable peeler, and sink them in a huge bowl of ice water. They will curl up and look like three times as much.

For cooked carrots, overcook them and see the recipe for what to do with overcooked carrots. Or mix them with peas (say, there's an original idea), broccoli plus cheese sauce, or Lima beans.

Old
For raw carrots, soak them in ice water overnight. Add the juice of 1 lemon or 1 tablespoon of vinegar to the water before soaking.

For cooked carrots, add a pinch of sugar and ¼ teaspoon of salt to each cup of cooking water.

Overcooked
Try making:

Bobbi's Carrot Casserole
Mash carrots with potatoes. (Quick, where're the instant mashed potatoes?) Pile into a casserole, top with cheese, and place under the broiler until the cheese melts.

See also the soup suggestion under ASPARAGUS, *Overcooked.*

Thawed
See Appendix B, regarding foods that have been thawed out before you wish to use them.

Too many

Aw, come on. Carrots keep almost a month when wrapped well in plastic wrap or foil. You're bound to think of something in 30 days.

If, however, they're already scraped, why not nibble them, with a dip to dunk them in, before dinner? Or make a carrot salad for tomorrow's dinner. You're having carrot salad today? Then cook them and see the next paragraph.

With a surplus of cooked carrots, consider the following:

Dilly Carrots

Marinate 4 cups of carrots overnight in French dressing (equal parts of oil and vinegar and 1 teaspoon of dillseed or weed or ¾ teaspoon of fresh dill). Add a dash of celery seed if you are so inclined.

Are you feeling really experimental? Make this:

Indian Carrot Pudding

Drain the carrots well. Mash them with ¼ cup of butter for every 2 cups of carrots and a little cream or milk if necessary to reach mashed-potato consistency. Now add 1 tablespoon of lime or lemon juice, 2 heaping tablespoons of chopped nuts (any kind), and 2 tablespoons of raisins. Sweeten until it tastes good to you (start with 2 tablespoons of sugar). Add ⅛ teaspoon of almond extract if you think it would help. You can serve this hot or cold, topped with whipped cream. Talk about pumpkins and squashes at dinner, and see if anyone figures out what you really made the dessert from. (They won't.)

Wilted: see CARROTS, *Old*

CATCHUP: see SAUCES

CAULIFLOWER

Bland

Two seasonings that go interestingly with blah cauliflower are

mace (sprinkle on a pinch) and p‹
teaspoons per head).

Burned
See Appendix A, regarding burned foo

Discoloring
If the cauliflower isn't as white as you'‹
vinegar after the water boils; it will whiter

Frozen to box
Run some cold water from the tap into the
flower will be liberated from its cardboard p‹

Not enough
Cooked cauliflower is a strange-shaped (caulifl‹
might say) vegetable that doesn't really toss
thing. But you can put any other vegetable (‹
bottom of a greased baking dish, then a layer ol
sort, then a layer of cauliflower, and then pour
sauce (white, cheese, even hollandaise) over the
tablespoon of the other vegetable as a garnish on

Old
Add a pinch of sugar and another pinch of salt to
every cup of water you use in cooking it. They will h
sweetness, flavor, and color.

Overcooked
Let us tell you about overcooked cauliflower: It is a god
dieters. You know all those things you make with white
(casseroles, gravies, timbales, etc.)? You can make awfully
facsimiles with overcooked cauliflower.

Keep cooking it until it is completely soft when you pok
with a spoon. Then mash it absolutely smooth. (A blen
does this quickly.) Add butter, or margarine, or milk until y
have the consistency of loose mashed potatoes.

Save this glop in the refrigerator to combine, for example
with turkey or roast drippings for lovely, guiltless gravy. Quite
good, too, on real mashed potatoes.

r make:

Mock Potato Puff

son the mashed cauliflower with onion powder, salt, and
pper. Pour into a baking dish, and top with Parmesan cheese.
ke ½ hour at 350°.

lty

cauliflower is too salty on the plate, put it back in clean,
ew boiling water for 1 minute.

If you oversalt the cooking water, change it at once.

Smelly

There are many who hold that most of the smells that emanate
from a cooking cauliflower come from the water. And most of
the smells enter the water during the first 5 minutes of boiling.
The solution, therefore, is to change the water after the cauliflower has boiled for 5 minutes.

If it is too late for that, toss a piece of bread (preferably rye)
into the pot. Or make a solution of 1 part vinegar to 3 parts
water, dip a cloth in it, wring it out, and spread it over the
top of the pot while the cauliflower cooks. Be careful not to let
the cloth catch fire from the burner.

Thawed

See Appendix B if your frozen cauliflower defrosted itself when
you weren't looking.

Too much

Raw cauliflower keeps.

Cooked cauliflower can be used in salads the next day. Or
cover it with plastic wrap and refrigerate for 2 or 3 days, and
then make:

Honey-Cheese-Glazed Cauliflower

Put the cauliflower in a pie plate. Spread it out, and fluff it up
so the glaze can dribble between the flowers. Drizzle 1 tablespoon of honey for each cup of cauliflower, and sprinkle a hand-

ful of shredded American cheese over it. Bake in a preheated 400° oven for 10 to 15 minutes—until the cheese is completely melted.

CELERY
Bland
Raw celery is vastly improved by filling the trough with some sort of delectable cheese goo—like this one: caviar (red or black; cheap or good) with sour cream or cream cheese plus a bit of Roquefort cheese. Soften it with milk if it is too stiff.

Cooked celery is perked up nicely if you add mustard or poppy seed to the cooking water.

Old: see CELERY, *Soggy*

Soggy
Soak wilted celery stalks in ice water for 2 to 3 hours. Option: Add 1 tablespoon of vinegar or the juice of 1 lemon to the water. Some say it helps retain the flavor.

An alternative: Wash the celery, and stand it vertically for 2 hours in a pitcher of cold water plus 1 teaspoon of salt, in the refrigerator.

Here is one of the world's only recipes specifying as an ingredient hopelessly soggy celery:

Pam Golden's Soggy Celery Dish
Trim the leaves. Poach old and hopelessly soggy celery (see!) in one can of consommé plus ½ cup of water for 10 minutes. Drain. Split the stalks in half. Cover them with French dressing. Chill in the refrigerator at least 4 hours, preferably 8, before serving.

CEREAL
Bland
Oh, my goodness, everything under the sun can be stirred into or sprinkled onto hot or cold cereals to make them more interesting. Just for starters:

Make hot cereal using chocolate milk instead of regular milk.

Add 1 teaspoon of cinnamon, a dash of ginger, or a few cloves to hot water before adding the cereal.

Stir a cup of canned chopped fruit (per 4 servings) into hot cereal halfway through the cooking process.

Add prunes, dates, raisins, currants, nuts, or other dried fruits to hot or cold cereals. Plump dried fruits into hot water and let stand 3 minutes for the fruit to rehydrate. Let cool before adding to cold cereal.

Put 1 tablespoon of jam in a bowl, add a bit of milk, mush them together, and add the cereal, hot or cold.

Put chocolate bits into oatmeal. (Think about chocolate-chip oatmeal cookies.)

Eat cold cereal with eggnog or instant malted milk.

Sweeten cereals with brown sugar or maple sugar or maple syrup or fruit sundae syrups.

Add ice cream, maraschino cherries, marshmallows, or vanilla.

Go really nuts. Serve a tossed salad with a bland type of dressing (like creamy French), and pour a lot of breakfast cereal, like Kix or Cheerios or Chex, onto it like croutons.

Loose
Add more cereal.

Lumpy
Push it through a strainer. This will probably make it loose. See CEREAL, *Loose*. Next time start with cold water and stir constantly, if you think it is worth the effort.

Soggy
To unsog soggy or limp cold cereal, pour it on a cooky sheet, and bake it for 2 or 3 minutes at 350°.

CHARD: see GREENS

CHEESE

Dried out, stale
If it is extremely hard, consider grating it (any cheese can be

grated), and use it on vegetables, in eggs, in soufflés, on scalloped potatoes, etc.

If it is dry but not all that dry, slice off the crusty edges (you can grate those), and either coat the bare edges with melted butter or wrap the whole cheese in a cloth which has been dipped in vinegar and wrung out. (Do you suppose that's what cheesecloth is really for?) Store in the refrigerator in either case.

Moldy

Cut off the moldy parts; the rest of the cheese won't be affected. To prevent mold from recurring, wrap the cheese tightly in a plastic bag.

Note: Please do not try to remove the mold from Roquefort or Bleu cheese. It is supposed to be there. Thank you.

Oily

Wrap the oily cheese in paper towels; they will absorb much of the excess oil within 3 days or so. When the towels become too oily, change them.

Rubbery, tough, stringy

This happens when there is too much heat. The excessive heat separates the fat from the protein in the cheese, and the result is a Welsh rabbit (or whatever) that is rubbery, tough, stringy, and often separated-looking.

This time dump the rabbit in a blender, and blend for a minute or so at low speed to break down the rubberiness. Pour it back into the pan or, better yet, into the top of a double boiler, and continue cooking. If the blending made it too loose, add some browned flour (flour that you have browned on a cooky sheet in a 400° oven) until it is the proper consistency.

Next time cook the rabbit from the start in the top of a double boiler, making sure the bottom of the top pot isn't touching the boiling water below. Then, unless Junior poured some rubber cement into the pot when your back was turned, you should have a perfect rabbit.

Soft; hard to cut
1. Heat the knife.
2. Go out and buy a cheese-cutting gadget for two bits at the five-and-ten.

Too much supposed-to-be-moldy cheese
Combine leftover Bleu or Roquefort cheese with an equal amount (by weight) of sweet butter, add a dollop of cognac, and store in a covered jar in the refrigerator. It lasts forever, and it's great on crackers as an hors d'oeuvre.

CHERRIES
Bland
For pies especially, it is nice if the cherries really taste like cherries. Surprisingly enough, they do even more so if you add a few drops of almond extract to them. This is primarily for canned cherries but works with fresh ones as well.

Pale
In cherry pies you want the cherries to be a nice bright red. If nature didn't do it, cheat a little and add red coloring to whatever you use as the thickening agent.

Pits
If you don't have a Tom Swift Steam-Powered Automatic Cherry Pitter, you can use a hairpin. Press the rounded top of the hairpin (or a paper clip) into the cherry at the stem end, then down under the pit, and lift up. Pin and pit should emerge leaving the cherry virtually unharmed.

Too many
Maybe now is the time to discover preserving foods. Cherries are just about the easiest fruit to handle and, therefore, a good beginning lesson in your self-taught course in canning or freezing. Just think about cherries jubilee or hot cherry pie in the middle of the winter. Home-frozen cherries last up to a year. Consult any big cookbook for step-by-step instructions.

CHESTNUTS: see NUTS

CHICKEN: see POULTRY

CHICKEN LIVERS: see LIVER

CHIPPED BEEF

Not enough
Stretch it by adding shredded Cheddar cheese to creamed chipped beef and serving it over biscuits instead of over toast.

Salty
Parboil it (which, in the case of chipped beef, means dunking it in boiling water for about 5 seconds).

CHOCOLATE AND COCOA

Have one, need the other
Three tablespoons of cocoa and 1 tablespoon of shortening may be substituted for 1 square of unsweetened chocolate. Or vice versa.

Scum or skin on surface
Remove it with a cold spoon; then float a marshmallow on the top to keep scum from reappearing.

Stuck to pan
There is nothing you can do about it now. Next time grease the pan very lightly, or use a double boiler.

CHOCOLATE SAUCE: see SAUCES

CLAMS: see also MUSSELS

Can't open
There is a long and involved procedure used by the purists. You may be blackballed from the Clam Fanciers League for the following, but it works nicely, thank you: Drop the clams 4 at a time into boiling water. After 15 seconds, remove and slip

a knife in between the shells. The water relaxes the muscle that is holding them shut.

Sandy, gritty
Sprinkle the clams with lots of corn meal. Then pour on enough water to cover them. Then wait 3 hours. They will have expelled the sand and grit. Wouldn't you in a similar situation?

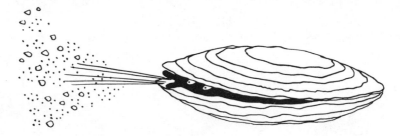

Uncertain quality
It is always safest to buy clams in the shell. Be suspicious of broken shells or ones that aren't tightly closed. Also discard any that float.

COCOA: see CHOCOLATE AND COCOA

COCONUTS

Can't open
Bake the coconut for 20 minutes at 300°. By the end of this time, either it will have cracked itself open, or a light tap on the (coconut's) noggin will do the job.

Dried up
Put the coconut meat in a bowl, cover it with cow's milk, and refrigerate for 1 hour. Press the meat dry in a strainer. The milk can then be used for drinking or cooking.

Or, if you have the time, put the coconut meat in an airtight place with a slice of fresh bread for 3 days, at the end of which time you will have fresh coconut and stale bread.

Stale shredded coconut

Method 1: Soak it in cow's milk plus a dash of sugar for 3 minutes.

Method 2: Hold it in a sieve over boiling water until it is as moist as you would like.

COFFEE

Cloudy

Add eggshells to the coffee while it is heating.

Not enough

Company's coming any minute, and you're nearly out of coffee. Make mocha, and you can serve 6 people with 2 cups of coffee. Here's how:

Mocha

Add ⅓ cup of cocoa and 3 cups of warmed milk (be careful not to let the milk boil) to 2 cups of coffee. Sweeten to taste (start with ¼ cup of sugar). A glug of rum or brandy and a flurry of cinnamon can turn a potential disaster into an occasion.

For after-dinner disasters, try *Café Brûlot*. Three cups of coffee will serve 6 people:

Café Brûlot

Drag out the chafing dish, or herd everyone into the kitchen; this is too spectacular to be missed. Into the chafing dish, put 6 ounces of brandy (or a mixture of rum and brandy, if you're low on brandy), 6 cloves, 6 teaspoons of sugar, and a few strips of orange peel. Heat the whole thing, and when it's nice and hot, ignite the vapors. Slowly add the 3 cups of coffee, stirring as you do so. Serve in your smallest cups; this is supposed to be a demitasse.

Overcooked

A tiny pinch of salt is said to take away the bitter taste of overcooked coffee.

Too hot
If you overheat coffee regularly, why not keep a small bowl of frozen coffee ice cubes in the freezer?

COLESLAW: see CABBAGE

CONSOMMÉ: see SOUPS

COOKIES
Bland
After baking (and tasting) the cookies, try sprinkling on small amounts of anise seed, cumin, cinnamon, ginger, or nutmeg. Or spread them with peanut butter and top with cake decorations or fancies. Or make sandwich cookies: Use any kind of jam or fudge for a filling. Or make:

Orange Cream-Cheese Frosting
Combine 3 ounces of cream cheese with 1 tablespoon of orange juice and 1 teaspoon of vanilla extract. Add 3 cups (yes, 3 cups) of sifted powdered sugar gradually, beating constantly. Spread on cookies.

Or brush the tops of bland cookies with 1 egg white beaten until foamy with 1 tablespoon of good sweet sherry, and sprinkle with slivered almonds. Broil for 1 minute to set the nuts.

Or glue a flat chocolate wafer (a nonpareil) to the middle of the cookies with a dot of frosting.

Crisp
Cookies that are too crisp will usually decrisp themselves if stored in an airtight container for at least 24 hours.

Crumbly dough
If cooky dough is too crumbly to roll easily, but you don't want to add more moisture, try letting the dough stand at room temperature for ½ hour.

Hard

Cookies that are too hard will soften if stored in an airtight container with something from which they can absorb moisture. A glass of water does nicely; so does a slice or two of fresh bread.

Spreading problems

If cooky dough doesn't spread out satisfactorily before or during baking, take something cold and smooth and flatten out each cooky with a rotary motion. Suggested cold and smooth thing number 1: a spoon dipped in cold water. Suggested cold and smooth thing number 2: an ice cube wrapped in smooth cloth.

Stuck to cooky sheet

Run the sheet or tin over a hot burner on the range. Or wrap the whole works in a towel as it comes hot from the oven, and let it stand for 5 minutes. Sometimes greasing the spatula helps.

Stuck to hands

Wash your hands in cold water. Or juggle a handful of ice cubes for as long as you can bear it. The dough won't stick.

Stuck to rolling pin

If you don't want to add more flour to the dough by flouring the pin, chill the pin in the freezer, and the dough won't stick.

CORN

Discoloring

Some people think light-yellow corn tastes better than dark-yellow corn. To fool such people, add a dash of vinegar to the water the corn is boiling in, and the corn will turn at least a few shades lighter as it cooks.

Not enough

You have 4 ears of corn and a fifth person shows up for dinner. Quick, make the most filling, fattening extra dish you can think of that goes with the main course. A bucket of biscuits with butter and honey will do nicely. Or Lima beans with butter and brown sugar stirred in. *Then* chop each ear of corn in half, and pile them in a vegetable dish. Some people will take 1, some 2, some 3. But no matter what, there will always be precisely 1 piece left when dinner is over. (Did you think we were going to suggest succotash? We don't think you need *that* much help.)

Old, not sweet

Any corn that has been thoughtfully prehusked for you by your well-meaning supermarket probably fits into this category. Before you cook it, slice a small piece off, and stand the ears on end in an inch of water for ½ hour or so.

Whether or not you presoak, try adding ½ cup of sugar to every 2 quarts of cooking water. A tablespoon or two of corn syrup will have the same beneficial effect.

Overcooked

It is hard to imagine, in our day and age, when you can buy frozen corn on the cob that tastes nearly as good as mush on a stick, that someone in your family is going to bite into a steaming ear of fresh, sweet, hot buttered corn and say, "Good grief, Sarah-or-whatever-your-name-is, you've overcooked the corn again."

If you feel guilty, however, give in and make fresh corn soup. The amount of work will surely absolve you.

Fresh Corn Soup

Cut the kernels from the cobs. For each cup of kernels, take 1 tablespoon of butter; melt in a heavy saucepan with 2 tablespoons (per cup) of chopped onion; add 1 tablespoon (per cup) of flour; and cook over a medium burner for 3 minutes, stirring constantly. Stir in the corn and 1 cup (per cup) of whole milk. Warm the milk first to avoid lumps. Warm the mixture thoroughly. Season to taste with salt and pepper, and serve with a tiny sprinkling of nutmeg.

Silky

Corn silks can often easily be removed simply by holding the ear under a hard stream of water from the faucet. The corn's ear, that is, not your own. Flick off the few remaining silks with a knife.

For more stubborn silks, a damp paper towel or even a whisk broom may be successfully employed.

Thawed

Please see Appendix B for remarks on thawed foods that you wish were still frozen.

Too much

Except in emergencies, corn on the cob should never be reheated; it toughens the corn. Here is a simple yet interesting recipe for leftover corn on the cob:

Delaware Corn Pudding

Scrape off all the kernels. Mix a cup of kernels with ¾ cup of bread crumbs, ½ cup of milk, 1 egg yolk, ½ green pepper (minced), plus salt and pepper. Fold in a stiffly beaten egg white. Put 2 strips of bacon on top, and bake at 350° for 30 minutes. Serves 2.

CORNED BEEF

Bland

Four different seasonings, alone or in concert, will successfully unbland bland corned or boiled beef. Try dillseed, a 1-inch stick of cinnamon, whole celery seed, or 4 or 5 whole allspices, added to the cooking water from the beginning.

Tough

You haven't cooked it long enough. Just keep going. It takes a long, long while to get some corned beef tender, but it eventually happens.

CORNSTARCH

Have none, need some

For most cooking purposes, you can substitute 2 teaspoons of flour for 1 teaspoon of cornstarch.

CRAB: see FISH AND SEA FOOD

CRACKERS

Not enough

Toast any kind of bread until dark. (Brown, not sunset.) Using a knife with a serrated blade, saw the bread in half the hard way, making 2 full-sized thin slices instead of 1 regular one. Cut in quarters. Instant (nearly) crackers.

Soggy

Put soggy crackers on a cooky sheet, and bake for 2 or 3 minutes at 350°.

CRANBERRIES: see BERRIES

CREAM: see also WHIPPED CREAM; SOUR CREAM

Have none, need some

Baking soda sweetens sour cream. So add a pinch of soda to some sour cream, and keep adding it slowly until the cream reaches the desired degree of sweetness. Start with a tiny, tiny pinch. A teaspoon per pint is the most you'd ever want to add, and rarely that much.

Or you can use powdered milk made by using less water than usual, or by adding milk to the powder instead of water.

Souring

Add a pinch of baking soda to sweeten souring cream.

CREAM PUFFS

Beads of moisture

This happens when cream puffs are underbaked. Return them to the hot oven, turn off the oven at once, and let them sit 5 minutes with the door ajar. The beads of moisture should disappear.

Collapsed

Cream puffs collapse when they are cooked on the outside and moist on the inside. So slice off the top, remove the moist dough with your fingers (yes, you can eat it), replace the top, and return to the hot oven. Turn the oven off, leave the door ajar, and wait 10 minutes. Then proceed normally.

CREAM SOUP: see SOUPS

CRISCO: see FAT, LARD, SHORTENING

CROQUETTES

Won't firm up

There are few things worse than a flabby croquette. Soak 1 teaspoon of gelatin in 2 tablespoons of cold water, and then dissolve it over boiling water. Stir it into the croquette mix, and wait until the gelatin hardens. The heat of cooking will dissolve the gelatin, and the croquette will be soft and creamy inside.

CUCUMBERS

Bland

Maybe what they need is dillseed. Try sprinkling some on sliced or marinated cucumbers or in cucumber salad. Or maybe celery seed.

Soggy, wilted

Put the cucumbers, whole, in a basin of cold water in the refrigerator. About an hour before you want to eat them, peel and slice them, sprinkle with salt, and put back in the water in the refrigerator. Drain before serving.

As an alternative, you can make:

Bulgarian Cucumber Soup

(There are lots of soggy cucumbers in Bulgaria.) Mix together 1 cup of plain yoghurt for each ½ to 1 cup of sliced cucumbers. Season to taste with salt, pepper, and a few pinches of sugar. Add a like quantity of dill.

Too many

If the cucumbers are nice, firm, unshriveled, and dark green, they will keep at least a week. If they are nasty, soft, shriveled, and light brown, you'd better hurry up and make this Norwegian dish:

Baked Stuffed Cucumbers Bergliot

Boil cucumbers for 5 minutes, unpeeled. Split them lengthwise, remove the seeds, and stuff with chopped-up leftover meat of any sort plus cheese and bread crumbs. Bake at 350° for 30 minutes.

Or you can simply sauté cucumbers. Slice them fairly thick—say ½ inch or so—bread them if you wish, and sauté until brown. Turn over and brown the other side. Serve with cheese sauce.

CUPCAKES: see CAKE

CURRY POWDER: see HERBS, SPICES, SEASONINGS

CUSTARDS: see PUDDINGS AND CUSTARDS

DATES
Stuck to each other
Toss them in a warm oven for a few minutes, and they should unstick.

Stuck to utensil
Next time dip the utensil (scissors or knife, probably) in cold water, and cut the dates while it is wet.

DISHES: see Appendix H: PROBLEMS WITH UTENSILS

DRINKS, ALCOHOLIC: see ALCOHOL

DUCK: see POULTRY

EGG WHITES
Won't whip
The eggs should be at least 3 days removed from the chicken. If you got them at a supermarket, they probably are. They should also be at room temperature. Either let them sit for ½ hour, or dunk them in lukewarm water for 5 minutes.

The beaters must be very clean and free of grease; even a tiny bit may retard whipping.

And if you've done all that and they still won't whip, add a pinch of baking soda or (less desirably) a pinch of salt. The whites may be a bit fluffier than usual, but they will whip.

EGGPLANT

Bland

There are some of us who feel that the best way to improve an eggplant is to encase it in cement and drop it in the river. Via secondhand knowledge, then, here are some seasonings that are alleged to improve the flavor of a bland eggplant: basil, celery seed, chervil, oregano, sage, and thyme. If you're breading, put the spices in the breading. If you're frying, sprinkle on before cooking.

Discoloring

If a sliced eggplant should start to discolor, drop it in salt water to retard the discoloration.

Hard to peel

If you wish to remove the skin from your eggplant to fry it or something, try slicing it first and then cutting the skin off the slices with a pair of scissors.

EGGS, GENERAL: see also EGG WHITES; EGGS, BOILED; EGGS, DEVILED; EGGS, FRIED; EGGS, POACHED; EGGS, SCRAMBLED

Cold
Eggs should be at room temperature for baking. To bring an egg from refrigerator temperature to room temperature quickly without cooking it in the process, dunk it in lukewarm water for 5 minutes.

Dirty
Dirty eggs are not a problem; clean eggs often are. When you wash eggs, you remove a protective coating, thoughtfully provided by the chicken, and they tend to spoil faster and to absorb refrigerator odors. If you must have clean-looking eggs, wipe them with a dry cloth. As a rule, it is best not to run raw eggs through the washing machine.

Dropped on the floor
Cover the mess with lots of salt. Let it stand for 20 minutes. If the dog hasn't lapped it up by this time, the whole works should sweep up easily with a broom and dustpan. (Anyone with a good recipe for *very* salty eggs, please get in touch with authors.)

Eggshell in egg
Probably the simplest way to remove bits of eggshell from eggs is to use the empty half eggshell as a scoop.

Not enough
In baking, you can generally replace about 1 egg in 3 with 1 tablespoon of cornstarch. Also, for most purposes, 2 yolks will substitute for 1 entire egg.

Overcooked
Overcooked fried, poached, scrambled, and other such eggs tend to be tough. So why not continue cooking them until they are totally overcooked, and then use them instead of hard-boiled eggs in salads, sandwiches, and the like?

Now, if your problem is that the breakfast eggs have overcooked and everyone is sitting there clamoring for breakfast, there is still hope. Make:

Baked Eggs Nora MacLean

Put the eggs in a baking dish (peel and slice them if hard-boiled). For 4 eggs, warm up a sauce made of a small can of white or cheese sauce plus ½ teaspoon of Worcestershire and 1 tablespoon of sherry. Pour the sauce on the eggs. Sprinkle with croutons (or shredded toast) and any kind of grated cheese. Bake for 10 minutes at 325°. Sprinkle with parsley flakes just before serving. Smile.

This recipe works best with overboiled and overpoached eggs. It will still work with overfried eggs, but they're not so glamorous. So smile prettier.

Stuck to carton
Wet the carton; the eggs will come out without cracking.

Stuck to egg beater, pots, etc.
The secret to cleaning eggs off utensils is to use cold water, not hot water.

Yolk in white
When you separate eggs and there are bits of yolk in the white, it is important to remove them, because the whites may not whip unless you do so. Remove the yolk with a yolk magnet, consisting of a cloth moistened in cold water. Touch it to the yolk, and it will cling.

EGGS, BOILED

Cracked before cooking
Wrap the egg very tightly in aluminum foil, twisting the ends. Then boil normally. After boiling, plunge quickly into cold water. If you don't, it will continue to cook in the foil.

Cracked during cooking
Pour in 1 teaspoon of salt; it should keep the whites from seep-

ing out. A few drops of lemon juice or vinegar in the egg water will have the same effect.

Crumbly; hard to slice
If you don't have an egg-slicing gadget, the easiest way to slice hard-boiled eggs is either to use a cheese slicer or to garrote the egg with thread. Or you can use a hot, dry knife.

Discoloring
Dark circles around the yolks of newly hard-boiled eggs can be prevented by cooking the eggs properly: Cover eggs with cool water to a height of 1 inch above the tops of the eggs. Bring rapidly to a boil. Take the pan off the heat, cover, and let stand for 20 minutes. Cool immediately in cold water.

If the eggs already have dark yolks, remove the darkness by holding the yolk under a gentle stream of cold water and lightly rubbing the yolk with your finger.

EGGS, DEVILED

Bland
Try adding crushed basil, cumin, curry, tarragon, and/or thyme to make deviled eggs a bit more devilish.

EGGS, FRIED

Grease splattering
Sprinkle cornstarch on the pan or griddle. This is said to impart a nice flavor to the eggs, as well.

Overcooked: see EGGS, GENERAL, *Overcooked*

EGGS, POACHED

Overcooked: see EGGS, GENERAL, *Overcooked*

Runny
A few drops of vinegar in the water will help keep poached eggs from running all over the pot.

EGGS, SCRAMBLED

Bland

In addition to all the "usual" stuff, like onions and mushrooms and tomatoes and spinach, consider the following seasonings, all of which are compatible with scrambled eggs: crushed basil, bay leaf, chervil, ground cloves, cumin, curry, marjoram, toasted poppy seed, rosemary, tarragon, thyme, and turmeric.

Overcooked

Continue cooking until they are all dried up. Then chop up to use on salads, for garnishes, or in egg salad.

FAT, LARD, SHORTENING

Hard to get out of can

When Crisco or other such fats get down toward the bottom of the can, fill the can with boiling water, cool it, and the shortening will float to the top, enabling you to utilize it down (up?) to the last drop.

Smelly

To remove odors from frying fat that you'd like to reuse, fry potato slices in it until they are brown. The potato will sop up all the extraneous odors—even powerful ones like fish and onion. (Why not do the potatoes last, and have a fish and chips dinner?)

Splattering

A dash of salt or cornstarch will often stop frying fat from splattering.

FIGS

Bland

Try powdered cinnamon or rosemary water (¼ teaspoon in ¼ cup of boiling water; remove from heat, let cool, strain out the rosemary, and pour the water onto the figs). Or stir ¼ teaspoon of powdered cardamon into ½ cup of honey and spoon over the figs.

Stuck together

When dried figs stick together, heat the whole shebang in the oven at 300° for a few minutes; they will come unstuck.

FISH AND SEA FOOD

Bland

Just about any herb or spice you have in the house can be used in some fashion on most fish dishes. Just to help you get started thinking about this, here is a partial list of relevant seasonings, with occasional comments:

Allspice (4 or 5 in the cooking water), anise (cod), basil (broiled or scalloped fish), bay leaf, chervil, cinnamon (bouillon), coriander (baked or broiled fish), curry, dill weed, fennel, garlic, ginger (broiled fish), mace (trout), marjoram (broiled, baked, creamed fish), mustard (fried, baked fish), nutmeg, oregano, paprika, rosemary (salmon), saffron (sauce), savory, sesame (fried, broiled, baked fish), tarragon (lobster, tuna, salmon), etc. etc. etc. Go wild.

Canny flavor

To make canned fish (crab, tuna, salmon, etc.) taste uncanny, soak it in fresh whatever-liquid-it-was-packed-in (either oil or water) for about ½ hour.

Gamy flavor

Some fish taste too gamy for some people. A sauce involving brandy, sherry, or ginger lessens the gaminess.

Overcooked

"When you overcook a fish," someone's grandmother must have said, "boil the hell out of it to make fish stock." Check your cookbooks for all the wondrous things to do with fish stock, among which is:

Sauce Velouté

Mix together 1 cup of fish stock, 2 tablespoons of butter, and 2 tablespoons of flour. You may add capers, mashed anchovies, or even a sardine for a little zing. Use on any fish right on the plate, or create a casserole by pouring the sauce over some bland cooked fish; add boiled sliced potatoes if you wish, and heat at 350° for 20 minutes.

Salty

When raw fish (or shrimp) is too salty, soak it in clear water for about 10 minutes. If you aren't going to serve it soon, store it in new water, not the water you just soaked it in.

Adding a lot of vinegar (1 cup per quart of liquid) to the cooking water helps cut down on saltiness while cooking fish.

Scaly

If an allegedly scaled fish still has scales on it, and you don't feel like hiking back to the fish store to trade it in, try plunging the fish into scalding water, then into cold water, and then scraping off the now-loosened scales with a serrated knife (like a grapefruit knife).

Smelly

In frying fish, the more dreadful smells usually come from the boiling fat, not from the fish itself. Reduce the heat, and see if it doesn't help.

When cooking fish in a pot, add some celery leaves to the pot. They will help destroy the fish smell (not entirely, however; who wants a fish that smells like celery?) and smell pretty good themselves.

In general, a caramel type of odor tends to neutralize fishy odors. So either issue caramels to your guests, or burn some granulated sugar in a pan. Either use a disposable pan or line a regular saucepan with aluminum foil.

Strong
Boiled fish sometimes comes out too strong. Let it stand in the cooking water or sauce after it is cooked, and the flavor will dissipate somewhat.

FLAMBÉED DISHES: see ALCOHOL, *Brandy or liqueur won't ignite*

FLOUR (ALL-PURPOSE)
Have none, need some
For 1 cup of all-purpose flour, you can substitute 1 cup plus 2 tablespoons of cake flour.

FOWL: see POULTRY

FRANKFURTERS: see SAUSAGES

FRENCH TOAST: see PANCAKES

FROSTING: see ICING

FROZEN FOODS: see specific foods; Appendix B

FRUIT: see specific fruit

FRUITCAKE: see CAKE

FUDGE: see CANDY

GARLIC
Hard to peel
If the peel is slightly loose, run hot water over the garlic, and the peel should come off readily.

If, as is usually the case, the peel is hard to get off, drop the garlic into boiling water for 5 seconds; then drop it in cold water. Now the peel should come off easily.

GELATIN

Stuck in mold
Loosen the gelatin around the edges with the tip of a knife. Dip the mold in hot water (not so far that the water runs onto the gelatin) for a few seconds, invert it on a plate, and shake the mold and the plate together in an up-and-down direction. Try to lift the mold off slowly. If it is still stuck, repeat. If it is *still* stuck, repeat again. If it is STILL stuck, you must have used library paste instead of gelatin powder.

Time is short
If you don't even have time to follow the "quick method" given on most boxes, try this "even quicker method," which may be up to 50 per cent faster. Add just enough hot water to the powder to dissolve it. A few tablespoons should be enough. Then use ice water for the rest of the liquid. If you add fruits, they should be very cold.

Too thick
If a gelatin dessert sets too long and you wanted to have stirred in fruits or marbles or something and you can't, warm it up by any convenient means (oven, stove, setting in a bowl of warm water) and it will thinen (which is the opposite of thicken). Then let it set again to the right consistency for stirring stuff in.

Too thin
If a gelatin dessert or salad won't thicken at all, or not fast enough for you, set it in an ice bath. An ice bath is a big bowl full of ice cubes.

GOOSEBERRIES: see BERRIES

GOULASH: see STEW

76

GRAPEFRUIT

Hard to get white stuff off

When you've peeled a grapefruit and there's still a lot of white stuff on it, you can either scrape at the white stuff with the edge of your serrated grapefruit knife, or you can dunk the grapefruit in hot water for 2 minutes. Next time boil the grapefruit for 5 minutes before peeling. All the white stuff will come away with the peel.

Hard to peel

Pour boiling water over the grapefruit, and let it stand for 5 minutes in the water. It should then peel readily.

Sour

Curiously enough, a bit of salt has the effect of making a sour grapefruit taste sweeter.

Unjuicy

If there are two of you (people, not grapefruits), stand at opposite ends of a large room, and roll the grapefruit back and forth for a few minutes. Rolling it around on a tabletop in a circular motion (like making balls out of clay) will have the same effect, although it is not nearly as much fun.

GRAVY

Bland, flat, pallid, gray

Depending on the kind of gravy, consider adding any of the following 4 kinds of ingredients:

1. Herbs and spices; for instance, ground allspice, coriander, marjoram, mustard, Kitchen Bouquet, savory, or thyme.

2. Extracts, such as bouillon cubes, yeast extract, or meat extracts.

3. Booze, of which sherry and port are most traditional, but white vermouth is an interesting variation.

4. Bottled mixed seasonings, such as soy sauce, Tabasco, Worcestershire, A1, and so on.

Fatty

If the fat is mostly on the top, you can either skim it off or sop it up with a piece of bread. If the fat is in the middle (and isn't that the case with most of us?), the easiest thing to do is to chill the gravy, skim the fat off, and reheat it.

Lumpy

Beat lumpy gravy with a whisk (not a whisk *broom;* a *whisk*) or with a rotary (hand-operated) beater; use a blender only as a last resort. Or pour (or force) the gravy through a wire strainer. Delumping gravy may make it too thin, in which case see GRAVY, *Too thin.*

Not brown enough

To darken gravy quickly without affecting the flavor, add 1 teaspoon of instant coffee.

Not enough

If there aren't enough leavings left in the pan to make any gravy at all, add 1 cup of water and a bouillon cube to whatever *is* in the pan, and cook until the cube is dissolved.

If you have some gravy but not enough, either add one of the many kinds of canned gravies available, or try this very fast substitute: For ½ cup of gravy, add 1 teaspoon of meat-flavored sauce (*e.g.*, Worcestershire or A1) and 1 teaspoon of lemon juice to one 8-ounce can of tomato sauce.

Salty
The only certain way to decrease saltiness is to increase quantity. A few pinches of brown sugar often have the effect of overcoming saltiness without sweetening. Or, for minor oversalting, cut up a raw potato in thin slices, and cook in the gravy until they become translucent.

Too thin
The best thickening agent is time. Not thyme, time. As a gravy cooks, the water evaporates, but not the other ingredients, so it becomes thicker. If you don't have time, or you can't afford to reduce the quantity, here are the most common thickening agents:

Arrowroot (about 1 tablespoon per cup of liquid, stirred in within 10 minutes of serving; can be done just before serving, because arrowroot has no taste of its own).

Cornstarch (about 1 to 1½ teaspoons per cup of liquid; allow time for gravy to cook and overcome the cornstarchy taste).

Other thickeners for various situations are rice, barley, a paste of flour and water (also good for scrapbooks and papier-mâché), milk, cream, egg yolks, mashed-potato flakes, and (ugh) blood: the blood of a bird or animal, preferably not the chef's, added just before serving. Here comes the most helpful hint in the last six pages: Never boil blood.

GREEN BEANS: see BEANS, LIMA AND STRING

GREEN ONIONS: see ONIONS

GREEN PEPPERS
Bland
Sprinkle with celery seed or a tiny bit (⅛ teaspoon per pepper) of fennel.

GREENS

Bland

For cooked greens, try adding one or more of these: mace, marjoram, or rosemary, to the cooking water, or sprinkling poppy seed or sesame seed on the finished product.

For raw greens, add anise (about ¼ teaspoon, crushed, per 4 servings), basil, chervil, caraway, or savory.

Dirty

Wash in warm water to loosen the dirt, eggs, nits, bugs, and worms. Now that you've learned what might have been in your greens, you've probably thrown them in the garbage and bought some canned lettuce. Fear not. Washing really works. (If they are especially dirty, you can even add some soap to the water.) Rinse in cold water—at least 4 rinses if you've used soap —until clean.

Hard to separate

If you can't separate the leaves of a lettuce or other tightly packed green vegetable easily, hit the stem end sharply on the counter; then twist out the core (it should come out easily if you hit it hard enough), and run cold water vigorously into the hole you have created. The leaves will separate beautifully, not unlike a green leafy peacock.

Rusting

If your lettuce or other greens are rusting, store them in a plastic bag along with a couple of paper napkins to absorb the moisture.

Smelly

If cooking greens get too smelly for your taste (or nose), add some salt to the cooking water, and cook uncovered.

Spinach is too spinachy

Nothing else is quite as spinachy as spinach. If your spinach is too spinachy, despinach it by adding some curry powder: about ½ teaspoon to a package of frozen spinach. If it still tastes bad, try a little crushed pineapple. Honest!

Wet

For regular loosely packed greens, let them drip into a colander; wrap them lightly in an absorbent towel, and chill. For Bibb and other full-headed greens, place them on a Turkish towel, cover with a plain towel, and chill for an hour or two.

If you need greens right away and they're wet, throw them in a pillowcase and spin them dry in your washing machine for a minute or two.

Wilted

If you've got an hour, dip the greens in hot water and then in ice water with a dash of vinegar. Shake the excess liquid from them, and chill in the refrigerator for 1 hour.

If you need them right away, unfatigue them by tossing with a few drops of oil to coat the leaves before adding dressing.

For hopelessly wilted greens, try this interesting recipe for hopelessly wilted greens:

Meredith's Hopelessly Wilted Greens Dish

Tear 2 heads or so of wilted greens into bite-size pieces. Make the following mixture: 4 slices of bacon, sautéed and chopped; ¼ cup of French dressing; ¼ teaspoon of celery salt; 2 tablespoons of chopped chives; 2 tablespoons of vinegar; 1 tablespoon of sugar; and boil it in the bacon skillet. Pour the sauce over the greens. Put the platter on top of a bowl of hot water, and steam for 6 minutes. Toss and serve.

HAM

Curling
If slices of ham are starting to curl under the broiler, slice the fat every inch or so.

Salty
Slice the ham. Soak the slices in milk for 15 to 30 minutes, then wash them off in cold water. This won't affect the taste of the ham at all, except by making it less salty.

HAMBURGERS

Bland
Mix any of the following seasonings in with the ground meat at a rate of roughly 1 or 2 teaspoons per pound: ground allspice, celery seed, cumin, garlic powder, nutmeg, oregano, or sesame.

If the hamburgers are already cooked and you want to do something more inspiring than drowning them in Store-bought Hamburger Sauce (*e.g.*, catchup), here are a few inspirations:

Cover them with gaucamole, pizza sauce, bacon crumbles, shredded Cheddar mixed with chopped walnuts, raisin sauce, curry sauce plus chutney, sautéed onions, sour cream plus horse-radish, a mound of diced stuffed green olives, or chili plus sliced black olives.

Or try one of these Truly Inspirational Hamburgers:

Hamburgers Bleu
Put a dollop of thick Bleu or Roquefort cheese dressing on the top. Add some crumbles of Bleu cheese and a strip of something red—like pimento or tomato. Broil for 3 minutes.

Hamburgers Pechter-San
To a small can of pineapple bits, add 1 tablespoon catchup (heaping), 1 tablespoon vinegar, and 1 teaspoon soy sauce.

Thicken with 2 teaspoons cornstarch dissolved in ¼ cup cold water. Heat until thick and gooey. Pour over hamburgers, and toss a few nuts on top.

Stuck to fingers
Dip your fingers in cold water first, and raw meat won't stick to them while you're molding meatballs or sculpting replicas of the Venus de Milo or whatever it is *you* do with ground round.

HANDS: see Appendix H, *Hands (your very own)*

HERBS, SPICES, SEASONINGS
Clogged
Salt shakers clog when the salt becomes moist. Overcome this problem by putting ½ teaspoon of raw rice or a tiny bit of blotter into the salt shaker. Or mix about 1 tablespoon of cornstarch into a normal-sized box of salt; it will pour freely.

Put about ½ teaspoon of whole peppers into a pepper shaker, and it will not only keep the pepper pouring; it will also impart a lovely fresh-pepper smell, if your nose can detect that sort of thing.

Old, weak
Many herbs lose their potency after a few months; most in a year. A satisfactory cure for impotency, however, is to soak them in hot water for 5 minutes, then in cold water for 5 minutes.

Some spices can be renewed, if it ties in with your recipe, by cooking them in butter for a few minutes before using. This method is especially effective with curry powder, for instance.

HOLLANDAISE SAUCE: see SAUCES

HONEY
Crystallized, sugared
Heating honey will restore it to its uncrystallized state, just the way it came out of the bee. A simple way to heat it is to stand the honeypot in a pan of hot water.

Have none, need some
In most recipes, you can substitute 1¼ cups of sugar and ¼ cup of any liquid for 1 cup of honey.

Stuck to container
Next time butter the container lightly before pouring the honey in; it won't stick at all.

HOT DOGS: see SAUSAGES

ICE CREAM

Icy
When ice cream stored in the freezer starts to get icy or crystallized, you can often cure the problem by wrapping it very tightly in aluminum foil and returning it to the freezer at least overnight.

Melted
It is probably safer not to refreeze melted ice cream, and if you do, it tastes pretty awful anyway. What, then, *do* you do with it? Here are a few suggestions:

Use it on fruit as a cream sauce, if the flavors seem compatible.

Pour it on chunks of toasted poundcake, for a Backward Cake Sundae.

Or save it in the refrigerator until tomorrow morning, and serve it with hot or cold cereal for breakfast; the kids will never forget it.

ICE CUBES

Air bubbles
International tensions are at an all-time high and you're worrying about air bubbles in your ice cubes? All right, next time boil the water first, pour it in the tray, let it cool to room temperature, and then put it in the freezer. No bubbles.

ICING

Gooey

Gooey icing is hard to spread unless you dip the knife in very hot water before spreading and again during the spreading process, as necessary.

Sugary

When boiled icing starts becoming sugary as it cooks, add a few drops of vinegar. This will retard the sugaring process but won't change the taste at all.

Too thick

If the icing is already made and too thick, stir in some cream until the consistency is right.

If it gets too thick while being made, beat or stir in a few drops of lemon juice or boiling water until it becomes thinner.

Too thin

Add sugar—preferably confectioners' sugar—a very little at a time, stirring madly or beating as you do so.

If, for some reason, you don't want to add sugar, beat the icing wherever there is indirect heat: in the hot sun, near an open oven door, or in the top of a double boiler.

JELL-O: see GELATIN

JELLY

Won't jell
Add the juice of a lemon or, if you have none, ¼ cup of white vinegar, and the jelly should jell.

Won't thicken
Put a grated carrot into a clean piece of cheesecloth. Squeeze a few drops of carrot essence into the jelly, and it is likely to thicken.

KALE: see GREENS

KETCHUP: see SAUCES

LAMB

Bland
Lamb is probably as compatible with as wide a variety of seasonings as anything in the supermarket. Consider, among others, the following: ground allspice, caraway seeds (especially in stew), chervil, cloves (add 5 or 6 to the marinade), coriander (sparingly—¼ teaspoon per 4 servings), cumin, dillseed, ginger, juniper berries (crush them and rub into the lamb), mace, oregano, rosemary, or tarragon.

Lamb chops curling
Slash the fat on the edges every ½ inch or so, and turn them over at once (you can turn them back later).

Mutton fat too strong
Mutton fat is great to cook with when it is not too strong. If it is too strong, add 1 part lard to 2 parts fat, chop it all up together, and melt in a double boiler with ¼ of its bulk in skim milk, with some sweet herbs (e.g., basil, marjoram, anise, or mint) thrown in.

Muttony
When lamb is too strong or too muttony, try the following demuttonizing marinade: Wipe lamb with a damp cloth and

86

rub with the juice of 1 lemon plus 2 tablespoons of olive oil. Let stand for 2 hours before cooking. Use garlic when you cook it.

LARD: see FAT, LARD, SHORTENING

LEMON

Dried up, old, unjuicy
Boil the lemon for about 5 minutes, and a lot more juice will come out. Roughly ⅓ more. (It is better, but not vital, to let the lemon cool in the refrigerator before juicing.) Heating for 5 minutes in a 300° oven will have the same effect. So, to a lesser extent, will rolling the lemon around on a tabletop with a circular pressing motion.

Pits falling in
Wrap half a lemon in cheesecloth before squeezing. For serving at dinner, the cheesecloth may be knotted or sewn shut. Very classy.

Squirting
The current world's record is held by a lady from Helena, Montana, who shot a stream of lemon juice 47 feet 3½ inches, or across the entire width of the dance floor of the Gilded Gazebo Supper Club. Good etiquette allows you to prevent squirting by inserting a fork into your lemon wedge and squeezing it over the fork, shielding it with your hand as you do so.

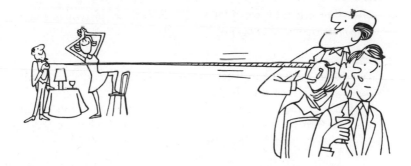

LETTUCE: see GREENS

LIMA BEANS: see BEANS, LIMA AND STRING

LIQUEUR: see ALCOHOL

LIVER

Bland

Liver, especially beef liver, isn't too compatible with herbs and spices, although caraway seeds and juniper berries (crushed and rubbed in) do have a pleasant effect. It is better to serve the bland liver with an appropriately yummy sauce; two for beef liver and one for chicken livers are given herewith:

Creole Sauce for Beef Liver

Mix together 8 ounces of tomato sauce, 2 tablespoons of vinegar, 1 tablespoon of brown sugar, ¼ cup of chopped onion, ¼ cup of chopped green pepper, and 1 minced clove of garlic.

Aunt Spo's Beef-Liver Sauce

Mix together ¾ cup of peanut butter (either smooth or chunky) which has been loosened with ¼ cup of boiling water; add 2 teaspoons of garlic salt, ⅛ teaspoon of cayenne pepper, and top with toasted sesame seeds, should you happen to have any.

Sour-Cream Sauce for Chicken Livers

Use 1 cup of sour cream for each pound of chicken livers. Season with 2 teaspoons of lemon juice and 1 teaspoon of chervil or dried dill weed, or with 1 tablespoon of tomato purée plus 1 teaspoon of oregano.

Cheap, tough

No matter what the instructions may say, meat tenderizer works as well on liver as on other sorts of meats.

If you anticipate that your liver is going to be tough or untasty, soak it for an hour in either milk or red wine, according to your taste, and fry in butter.

Popping, splattering
Chicken livers are wont to do this, but they won't if you perforate them all over with a fork.

LOBSTER: see FISH AND SEA FOOD

LOGANBERRIES: see BERRIES

MACARONI: see PASTA

MANGOES

Hard to peel
All mangoes are hard to peel from one end and easy to peel from the other. As the famous calypso song goes, "If your mango hard to peel, try the other end, my friend."

Unripe
Put unripe mangoes in a paper bag, and keep them in a dark, warm place until they ripen. Ripe mangoes are normally a bright yellow-orange.

MARGARINE: see BUTTER AND MARGARINE

MARSHMALLOWS

Hard, stale
Seal them up in an airtight place (like a plastic bag) with a slice of fresh bread for 3 days, and you will have fresh marshmallows and a stale slice of bread.

Stuck to utensil while cutting
Dip the scissors (you *were* using a scissors, weren't you?) in cold water, and cut while the blades are still wet.

MAYONNAISE

Curdled
Place 1 egg yolk in a clean, cold, dry bowl. Add the mayonnaise very, very slowly, stirring as you add.

Not enough

In things like egg salad or for sandwiches, stir in some catchup or chili sauce if the taste is compatible. If not, thin out the mayonnaise (see MAYONNAISE, *Too thick*), and increase the seasoning in the salad. Or look in your big cookbook for how to make more mayonnaise. It's unbelievably easy in a blender!

Separated

Rinse a bowl in hot water, and dry it. Add 1 teaspoon of prepared mustard, 1 teaspoon of mayonnaise, and beat with a whisk until creamy. Add another teaspoon of mayonnaise, and repeat. And so on, 1 teaspoon at a time.

Too thick

Thin it out with cream, whipped cream, evaporated milk, or lemon juice, whichever is handiest. None of these will flavor the mayonnaise. If you'd like to flavor it, you can thin it out with fruit juice. The juice from a cantaloupe or watermelon is especially interesting.

MEAT LOAF

Bland

All of these seasonings (used one or two at a time, please) go nicely with meat loaf: ground allspice, celery seed, coriander, fennel, garlic powder, nutmeg, oregano, paprika, and sesame seed.

Stuck to pan

This time scrape it out as best you can with a spatula and reassemble it, using sauce to hold it together.

Next time put a strip or two of partly cooked bacon underneath the meat loaf before cooking, and it will not only not stick, but it also won't taste bacon-flavored.

MERINGUE

Hard to cut

Dip the knife in very cold water.

Weeping

We hate to see a growing meringue cry. It tends to do so when it is cooled too fast. Cool it very slowly, by leaving it in the oven as the oven cools, for instance, and it will weep no more.

MILK

Have none, need some

If you don't have powdered milk on your emergency shelf, then for most uses (including drinking, but especially cooking) you can substitute the following for 1 cup of whole milk: 1 cup of buttermilk plus ½ teaspoon of baking soda; or 1 cup of skim milk plus 2 teaspoons of oil or fat. If you need sour milk, add 1 teaspoon of lemon juice or cider vinegar to 1 cup of regular milk.

Souring

Add 2 teaspoons of baking soda to a quart of milk, and it will be good for another day or two. This is the lactic equivalent of putting a penny in the fuse.

MOLASSES

Stuck to container

Next time butter the container lightly, and the molasses will roll right off.

MUFFINS: see BREAD, ROLLS, MUFFINS

MUSHROOM SOUP: see SOUPS

MUSHROOMS

Bland

The best seasoning to bring out the flavor in mushrooms is marjoram. Add a generous dash to cooking mushrooms. No marjoram? Have you got the thyme?

Darkening; too dark

Wipe them with a damp cloth, rub them with lemon juice, and

store them in the refrigerator. Or steam them in milk or butter in the top of a double boiler for 20 minutes. Or, while cooking, add a few drops of lemon juice to the cooking liquid. (It is just about impossible to lighten mushrooms in a black iron skillet.)

Shriveled
Peel them with your fingers. Beneath every shriveled mushroom there lies a somewhat smaller smooth mushroom waiting to be found. (Use the peelings to flavor soup or sauces.)

Too light
Mushrooms will darken if cooked in butter in a black iron skillet on high heat.

MUSSELS: see also CLAMS

Uncertain quality
Steam mussels for 10 minutes. If they open up, they're good; if not, they're not.

MUSTARD GREENS: see GREENS

MUTTON: see LAMB

NOODLES: see PASTA

NUTS

Crumbly
If nut meats crumble when you crack the shells, soak the remaining unshelled nuts in salt water overnight.

Hard to crack, shell, peel, remove nut meat, etc.
For almonds and similar nuts, drop the whole nut (shelled) in boiling water, and let stand for 3 minutes with the heat off. The skins should come off easily. Dry the nut meats on a towel.

For chestnuts and similar nuts, make a small gash on the flat side of the nut, penetrating the outer skin. Roast in a 400° oven until the skins loosen.

For pecans and similar nuts, cover them with boiling water,

and let stand until cold. Crack the nuts end to end with a nutcracker, and the meat should emerge in one piece.

Have none, need some

In brownies and other such, coarse bran can successfully be substituted for nuts.

In molasses cake, spice cake, and other stuff of that ilk, brown a cup of rolled oats, and add before baking.

Shells mixed in with nuts

Dump the whole works in a bowl of water. The shells will float, the meat will sink, and the guppies will swim around in the middle.

OATMEAL: see CEREAL

OLIVES

Hard to pit

Place them on a paper towel or wax paper. Roll gently with a rolling pin. Press the olive with the heel of your hand, and the pit will pop out.

ONIONS

Bland

Powdered basil, ginger, sage, and thyme are all good things to add to bland cooking onions. Or just butter and lightly sugar them.

Crying while peeling or slicing
The best antidote for most people is coldness. If you have time, chill the onions in the freezer for 10 or 15 minutes or more before slicing. Or peel them under cold running water. For some people, biting on a piece of bread seems to help; for others, not at all.

Falling apart while cooking (the onions, not you)
Mark an X on the root end of the onion with a sharp knife, and it will help hold loose onions together. (The root end is usually flatter, and it has a little dark spot where the root was.)

Hard to peel
Hot water loosens onion peels. Drop onions in boiling water for somewhere between 10 seconds (for tiny white onions) to 5 minutes (for big old red ones), and then dip them in cold water, and the peel will virtually fall off.

Sautéing unevenly
The recipe calls for browned onions, and some are dark brown while others are still white. Sprinkle the onions with a bit of sugar as they cook, and they should sauté evenly thereafter.

Smelly
Spicy smells tend to overcome oniony smells. The simplest spicy smell maker is a few cloves simmering in a pan of vinegar.

Too soft
Boiled onions that have become too soft can be firmed up again by dipping them briefly in ice water

Wilting
When green onions start wilting, you can revive them by re-planting them! Simply stick the root end in the ground, and it will take root and grow healthy again. This does not, alas, work with human beings.

ORANGES

Bland
Vanilla is delightfully compatible with orange flavor. Add a tiny bit of vanilla extract to your indifferently flavored oranges or to indifferently flavored orange juice as well.

Hard to peel
Pour boiling water over the oranges, and let them stand for 5 minutes. The peels will come off very easily, and so will all the white stuff under the peel. The peel is permanently loosened by this technique, so you can do it in advance and still refrigerate the oranges. This process also tends to make the oranges far juicier.

Unjuicy
See ORANGES, *Hard to peel*. Or roll the oranges around on a table, as if you were trying to make them rounder. That really loosens the old juices.

OYSTER PLANT: see SALSIFY

PANCAKES

Cold and soggy
Pancakes can be reheated without overcooking by placing them between the folds of a dish towel in a low (250°) oven.

Left over
There isn't a whole lot you can do with leftover pancakes. Make sandwiches. Cut them in strips and use as noodles. Or sail them around the back yard as Frisbees. Your choice.

Stuck to griddle
Usually means they aren't fatty enough. Next batch put in more shortening.

PANS: see Appendix H: PROBLEMS WITH UTENSILS

PARSLEY

Hard to chop
Wash it very briefly in hot water, and dry it off with paper towels. Its chopability quotient should rise noticeably.

PASTA

Boiling over
The immediate remedy is to blow on the surface of the water. This will give you about 15 seconds' grace period to look frantically around for the pot holders. If you can't find them, blow again. And again. Then put a bit of oil (about a tablespoon) in the water. Next time lightly grease the top inch of your pot.

Stuck together
After spaghetti or macaroni is drained and is stuck together, you can unstick it by reboiling it for about 2 minutes, and this time put a healthy glug of oil in the water. Next time put the oil in at the start, and the problem won't arise.

PEA SOUP: see soups

PEACHES

Darkening
Sprinkle them with lemon juice after peeling to retard the approaching darkness.

Fuzzy
Say, do you remember those television commercials where they used to shave a peach? If your peach is very ripe and very fuzzy, that may be your only solution. (Did anyone ever wonder about how to get peach fuzz out of an electric-razor mechanism?) For less ripe peaches, scrub them with a vegetable brush, and they will ripen into clean-shaven adult peaches.

Hard to peel
Firm peaches can be peeled just like potatoes, using a potato

peeler, which may then be called a peach peeler. Soft peaches can be peeled like tomatoes, which, as you know if you're reading this book from the rear, are peeled by soaking in boiling water, off the stove, for about 3 minutes.

PEANUT BUTTER

Separating
Turn the jar upside down, and put it back on the shelf.

Too thick
You can freeze the bread first, either if the sandwich isn't going to be eaten until later or if you happen to like frozen peanut-butter sandwiches. Or you can thin down the peanut butter with one of these four peanut-butter thinners: soft butter, maple syrup, hot water, or orange juice.

PEAS

Bland
All these five seasonings are said to pep up tired old peas: basil, marjoram, poppy seed, rosemary, and sage. Or combine with minced onions that have been browned in butter. You may call this dish Peas Lyonnaise.

Frozen to box
Run cold tap water into the spaces in the box, and the peas should come rolling out.

Thawed
See Appendix B to help you decide what to do about peas that have thawed out too soon.

Uncertain quality
Drop dried peas in water. The bad ones will float, and the good ones will sink to the bottom.

PECANS: see NUTS

PEPPER: see HERBS, SPICES, SEASONINGS

PERSIMMONS
Unripe
Here is an astonishing method for overnight ripening of unripe persimmons. The only reason it didn't make page-one headlines is that so few newspaper editors like persimmons. Wrap the unripe persimmon in aluminum foil. Put it in the freezer. When it is frozen solid, remove and allow to thaw at room temperature. When it is thawed out, it will be ripe. Stop the press!

PICKLES
Not pickly enough
Put them back in the jar with a bunch of dill, unless there already is dill in the jar. The longer they sit, the picklier they get, until eventually they may burn a hole right through the jar.

Scum on jar
Float 1 teaspoon of olive oil on the surface of the liquid in the jar, and the scum will go away and not return.

PIES: see also CAKE; COOKIES; CREAM PUFFS
Bland
Ground allspice is a fine pepper-upper for most kinds of pies, including apple, berry, raisin, pumpkin, prune, and custard, among others. Add ¼ teaspoon to the filling, to start with.

Caraway seeds in the crust give apple pie a different and interesting taste. Add 1 teaspoon per 2 cups of flour. Two other good things to add: cumin to the fruit of a fruit pie before putting on the top crust; fennel sprinkled on top of the crust before baking.

Drying out while cooking

Erecting a small smokestack in the center of the pie permits the heat to escape, so it doesn't stay inside and boil the juices away. The simplest sort of smokestack is a piece of raw macaroni inserted vertically right in the middle of the pie.

If the pie has already dried out too much, you can wet it by making a simple syrup, adding a dash of rum or cognac if it suits your fancy, and pouring it through the slashes in the crust.

(Oh, I thought you'd never ask. Simple syrup: ½ cup sugar into 1 cup water in a saucepan. Cover. Bring to a boil. Uncover. Simmer 3 minutes. Even simpler syrup: ½ cup water and ¼ cup currant jelly heated to boiling. Simplest syrup: syrup. Use maple syrup right from the bottle.)

Hot

The traditional way of cooling pies is putting them on window sills, from which they are stolen by small freckle-faced boys.

Now that the window sill is going the way of the running board, pies may be cooled quickly by putting a layer of ice cubes in a big pan and resting the pie tin on top of the ice cubes.

Soggy crust
Brush the sides and the top crust with beaten (but not fluffy) egg white, and put in a hot oven (400°) for 4 minutes.

Too sweet
Add the juice of ½ lemon to the filling. This also helps to bring out the flavor of the fruit, especially in berry pies.

PINEAPPLE

Canned flavor
Soak the pineapple slices or chunks in cold water for ½ hour to take away their "tin-can" taste.

Hard to peel
It can be difficult if you don't have one of those $3-billion machines they use in the pineapple factories. So how about slicing the pineapple first and then cutting away the peel and the core afterward? Much easier.

Unripe
Speed up the ripening process by sealing the pineapple in a brown paper bag and storing it in a warm (not hot) place. You'll know it's ripe when one of the center leaves pulls out easily.

PIZZA

Burned
It is almost always the crust and not the topping that gets burned. Scrape off the topping, and use it either on another pizza, on toast if you're in a hurry, or stirred into some sort of macaroni casserole.

Too gunky to cut
Sometimes pizzas are so gunky that even those circular pizza

knives don't work effectively. In such cases, try cutting the pizza apart with an ordinary kitchen scissors. (You can even use out-of-the-ordinary kitchen scissors, if that's what you have.)

PLATES: see Appendix H: PROBLEMS WITH UTENSILS

POPCORN

Won't pop

The usual reason is that it is too dry. Soak the kernels in water for 5 minutes, drain them, and try again.

If this doesn't work, an almost certain remedy is to freeze the kernels for 24 hours or more, and pop them while they're still frozen.

PORK

Bland

These seasonings go best with pork: caraway seeds, cardamon (about 1 teaspoon per 4 servings), chervil, cloves (4 or 5 in the marinade), coriander, cumin, fennel (rub ½ teaspoon into a roast), juniper, marjoram, oregano (mix with olive oil, and rub on a roast), paprika, rosemary, and sage.

Salty

If salt pork is too salty, blanch it for 2 minutes.

POT ROAST

Fatty

If your pot roast really looks too fatty to be acceptable, cook it well, chill it in the refrigerator, remove the now-solidified fat, and return to the pot or wherever it was.

Tough

In addition to the usual meat tenderizers, you might consider adding tomatoes to the pot the roast is roasting in. The acid in tomatoes breaks down the fibers in the meat, thereby tenderizing same.

If you don't have 3 hours to simmer it, slice it very thin, put it back in the pot for 15 minutes, and then serve.

POTATO CHIPS

Broken

Here is something mildly interesting to do with broken potato chips (more interesting than throwing them out, anyway): Use them as a casserole topping.

Soggy

Put them very briefly under the broiler; don't let them brown.

POTATOES

Baked: cold

Baked potatoes can be reheated without overcooking by dipping them in cold water and putting them into a 350° oven for 10 minutes.

Baked: exploding

This time duck! Next time cut a slice in the potato, or puncture it with a fork to let the steam escape, thereby preventing explosions.

Baked: fast method

Parboiling for 5 minutes before baking or sticking one of those potato nails (or any big aluminum nail) through the potato will cut the baking time by about 20 minutes. For really fast baked potatoes, wrap them tightly in foil, put them on a rack in a pressure cooker, add water to the level of the rack, and cook for 15 minutes.

Boiled: bland
Add a pinch of rosemary or a bay leaf to the cooking liquid. Or top them with sour cream to which you have added a pinch of marjoram.

Boiled: old and stale
Add a slice of lemon to the water; it tends to prevent discoloring and helps bring out what flavor remains.

Boiled: skin sticks to knife or hands while peeling
Dab a tiny bit of butter or other shortening on the knife, peeler, and/or hands, whichever it is that is troubled by having peels stick to it and/or them.

Mashed: bland
There comes a time in everyone's life, often at an early age, when he just can't stomach another spoonful of mashed potatoes. If you have just made a large batch when this phenomenon comes suddenly upon your family, try adding some nutmeg to the potatoes and frying them in butter. Not bad at all.

Mashed: won't fluff
Add a pinch or two of baking powder to the potatoes, and keep fluffing.

Not enough
But why don't you have mashed-potato flakes? God helps those who help themselves.

Roast: fast method
You say you're serving roast with potatoes and you forgot to put the potatoes in? All right, don't panic. Parboil them for 15 minutes, and add them to the roasting pan. They will be fully cooked in 45 minutes at 300°—a bit faster at higher temperatures or with smaller potatoes (or ones you've cut in half).

POTS: see Appendix H: PROBLEMS WITH UTENSILS

POULTRY
Batter falls off
Well, we know *why* it happened, but we don't know what to do about it. It happened because the bird wasn't dry before you dipped it in the egg or coating. Next time dry the wet little fellow with a towel before dipping, and let sit for 15 minutes between dipping and frying.

Bland
Try rubbing the bird with marjoram (which is also interesting in chicken salad). Mix oregano with olive oil, and rub it on the fowl. Likewise with rosemary or tarragon or thyme. Mix some hot mustard, oregano, paprika, or sesame seed in with the batter for fried chicken. Crush 3 or 4 juniper berries into chicken salad. And so on.

Dry
Turkey, in particular, can get so dry it makes your tongue fuzzy. Slice it, and arrange it on a heatproof platter. Make a sauce of half butter and half chicken broth. Pour it on the sliced bird, and let it stand in a 250° oven for 10 minutes to soak up the juices.

Feathery
In our modern age of convenience, most birds come defeathered.

In our modern age of deteriorating personal services, often the defeathering isn't good enough. If you don't have a chicken plucker on your household staff, here are two reasonably simple methods of defeathering a fowl:

1. The hot wax treatment: Add paraffin, or old candles, to boiling water. Wait until it melts. Dip the bird up and down in the pot until it is coated with wax. Wrap in newspaper and cool. Now, as you peel off the wax, the feathers should come off along with it. Or you can stick a wick up the bird's beak and have an emergency candle.

2. The soap method: Heat a big pot of water to boiling. Add ¼ cup dishwasher detergent. Drop the fowl in the water, slosh it around for a few minutes, and roll it up in a towel. You should be able to rub off any remaining feathers. Follow with a cool-water rinse, and don't worry about the taste—no soap.

Freezer burn
Dry spots on frozen fowl can and usually do mean freezer burn. Smell the creature carefully, and if you have any doubts as to its condition, junk it. If it smells all right, rub the skin with oil before roasting.

Frozen
Manufacturers usually recommend that frozen chickens and turkeys be defrosted slowly in the refrigerator—a process that

often takes 3 or 4 days. The main reason for this recommendation is that faster thawing causes the bird to lose juices and thus become tougher. You can overcome this to some extent by thawing it out in an airtight place, like a big plastic bag. If you're in a hurry, put the bag in a bowl of lukewarm water.

Gamy
Sometimes duck or pheasant or even turkey will taste too gamy for your palate. This is no reflection on the bird's behavior in the barnyard. Ginger, sherry, and brandy (the latter two applied to the bird, please) have a tendency to lessen gamy taste in poultry. You can rub ½ teaspoon of powdered ginger into the bird's skin before roasting or add any of the three to the gravy or sauce you serve over the meat.

Not enough
Serve the poultry on a waffle which you have made by adding 2 teaspoons of poultry seasoning to the batter before adding the liquid. You can get away with about half as much meat if you're lucky.

Tough
Meat tenderizer will work on fowl as well. For poultry cooked in liquid, try adding a pinch of baking soda to the liquid. And for those cooked with flame, tenderize the birds by rubbing them inside and out with lemon juice before cooking.

PRUNES
Bland
Add thin lemon slices while cooking your prunes.

Dry, tough
Cover them with boiling water. Put in the refrigerator overnight. This doesn't cook them; it just plumps them up.

PUDDINGS AND CUSTARDS
Bland
Toss a bay leaf or a pinch of ginger into almost any kind of

custard. Blah puddings can benefit from the addition of ground allspice, cinnamon, ginger, mace (especially in chocolate), and nutmeg.

Cold

Hot puddings and custards can be reheated without cooking them more by covering them with lettuce leaves and returning to a warm oven until you are ready for them.

Curdling

When pudding starts to curdle, the first thing to do is to stop it from cooking any further. Do this by hastily putting the pan in cold water; better still, ice water (this may be the origin of the Hastily Putting Club), and then beat with an egg beater or whisk until it is smooth again.

If the pudding or, especially, custard has already curdled, you can frequently uncurdle it with this time-consuming method: Add 1 tablespoon of custard to 1 teaspoon of milk or liqueur. Beat until creamy. Add the remaining custard 1 tablespoon at a time, beating each time until creamy. Then return to your recipe.

Skin is forming

If the taste is compatible, sprinkle 1 teaspoon of sugar on the surface. If it is not, put wax paper on the surface, and remove it when the pudding has cooled.

Too thin

For creamy puddings that are too thin, add any (not all) of the following for each cup of milk used: 3 tablespoons flour, 1 tablespoon cornstarch, 1½ tablespoons rice flour, 1 tablespoon arrowroot, or 1 tablespoon tapioca.

For molded puddings, add any of the following for each cup of milk used: 4 tablespoons flour, 1½ tablespoons cornstarch, 2½ tablespoons corn meal, or 2 tablespoons rice flour.

For soft custard, add 1 egg (or 2 yolks or 2 whites) for each cup of milk.

For molded custard, double the quantity of eggs, or use ½ tablespoon gelatin powder per cup of milk.

PUFF PASTE: see CREAM PUFFS

PUMPKIN: see SQUASH, SWEET POTATOES, PUMPKIN

PUNCH: see ALCOHOL

RABBIT, WELSH: see CHEESE, *Rubbery, tough, stringy*

RADISHES
Wilted, soft, soggy
Soak them in ice water for 2 to 3 hours. Option: Add 1 tablespoon of vinegar or the juice of 1 lemon to the water.

RAGOUT: see STEW

RAISINS
Shriveled
You can replumpify shriveled raisins by simmering them in just enough water to cover them, for 3 to 4 minutes. Say, aren't raisins *supposed* to be shriveled, though? Oh, well.

Sink to the bottom
If raisins are sinking to the bottom of your cakes or cookies or whatever, coat them lightly with flour and they will disperse themselves throughout the whatever, just the way you wanted. If what you are making is raisin upside-down cookies, ignore this.

Stuck together
Heat your congealed mass of raisins in the oven at 300° for a few minutes, and they will unstick themselves.

RASPBERRIES: see BERRIES

RAVIOLI: see PASTA

RHUBARB

Too tart

All rhubarb is too tart, some of us think. To detart it without adding absurd amounts of sugar, cut up the rhubarb and soak it for 3 minutes in hot water to which you have added a pinch of either baking soda or salt.

RICE

Boiling over

First, blow on the pan. This will cool the water down enough so that it will stop boiling over. For a longer-term preventive, toss a lump of butter in the pot; it cannot but help flavor the rice positively as well.

Burned

As soon as you discover you've burned the rice (again), turn off the flame, place the heel of a loaf of bread on top of the rice, cover the pot, and wait 5 minutes. Virtually all the scorched taste should disappear into the bread. Serve the rice to friends and the bread to enemies.

Cold

Reheat rice without overcooking by putting it in either a big sieve or a colander and placing it over a pan of boiling or simmering water (depending on how cold it is and how fast you need it). Keep the rice out of the water.

Not white enough

Are you sure it isn't brown rice? All right, add 1 teaspoon of lemon juice to the cooking water, and the rice will whiten.

Too much

You can reheat leftover rice (see RICE, *Cold*), but why not try something absurd, like:

Corky's Rice Fritters

Dissolve ½ package of dry yeast in ½ cup very warm (about 110°) water. Mix 1½ to 2 cups leftover lukewarm rice into the yeast. Cover it and let it sit overnight. Next day add 3 beaten eggs, 1 cup all-purpose flour, ¼ cup sugar, ½ teaspoon salt, and ¼ teaspoon cinnamon. Let it sit for another hour or so. Drop 1 teaspoonful at a time into hot deep fat (360°), and fry until golden brown. Sprinkle with confectioners' sugar, and serve with whipped cream or applesauce for a dessert or as an accompaniment to ham or chicken.

Uneven cooking
When rice is cooked on the bottom of the pot and raw on the top, it means too much steam is escaping. Give the rice a big stir (don't worry, Uncle Ben won't mind), cover the pot either with foil or with a Turkish towel (be sure to fold the loose ends up over the top), replace the lid, and keep cooking.

ROAST BEEF
Not enough
Slice the beef thinly, serve it over toast, and cover with a sauce. You can use cheese soup as a sauce if you like meat-and-cheese dinners; tomato sauce, made from a can of tomato soup (see the label on the can or your big cookbook for directions); hollandaise (you *have* completed your "first-aid kit," haven't you?); or add a pinch of tarragon to the hollandaise and you have Béarnaise sauce.

Overcooked
Cut off all unusable burned pieces, and slice the roast thinly. It will probably be dry and tough, in which case you can float it in a sauce (see ROAST BEEF, *Not enough*).

Too much
Go out and get Peg Bracken's *The I Hate to Cook Book*. We can't improve on her Beef Encore (otherwise known as Eiffel Trifle).

ROLLS: see BREAD, ROLLS, MUFFINS

RUM: see ALCOHOL

RUTABAGAS

Smelly

A recent national survey showed that .000000001 per cent of the population is troubled by smelly rutabagas. For you, madam, this advice: Add 1 teaspoon of sugar to the cooking water.

SALAD: see GREENS

SALAD DRESSING: see also SAUCES

Bland

One interesting way to pep up bottled store-bought French or Italian dressing is to put a halved clove in the bottle and let it stand overnight or longer.

SALSIFY

Darkening

The same lady who has smelly rutabagas also has darkening salsify. Store this herb in water to which you have added 2 tablespoons of vinegar or the juice of 1 lemon for each quart of water.

SALT: see HERBS, SPICES, SEASONINGS

SALT PORK: see PORK

SANDWICHES: see BREAD, ROLLS, MUFFINS; specific sandwich ingredients

SAUCES

Bland

Every herb, spice, seasoning, bottled flavoring, and kind of alcohol (any cooking kind, anyway) in your house can be used in sauces. There is no excuse whatever for a flat sauce. Consult your favorite cookbook, and get to work. And shame on you. (If you can't think of anything to do, add a dollop of sherry to any sauce whatsoever, and at least people will know you tried.) See also page 12 under *Two small cans or packages of hollandaise sauce* for suggestions on making quick Béarnaise, Choron, and Maltaise sauces.

Catchup won't pour

Put a soda straw down to the bottom of the bottle. It will pass enough air down to the bottom to permit the catchup to pour readily.

Curdled

Remove from the heat at once. For delicate sauces, like hollandaise, add an ice cube to retard further cooking. Beat hard with a hand beater or a whisk (having removed the ice cube). If necessary, strain it, too. Next time use a double boiler or lower heat, stir constantly, and add the fragile, curdle-producing stuff (eggs, sour cream, etc.) just before serving.

Fatty

Chill, skim off the fat, and reheat. For fast skimming, take off as much fat as you can with a spoon (tilt the pot so most of the juice will come up to the surface), toss in a few ice cubes, wait until the fat congeals on them, and remove. Then blot the last bits up with paper towels laid on the surface of the sauce. Reheat.

Lumpy

If you can, push the sauce through a strainer. If you can't, beat with a whisk or hand beater. Use electric appliances (beater or blender) only as a last resort.

Not enough

Whether your problem is too little liquid in a stew or not enough gravy for a roast, the solution is basically the same: Add more liquid to what you've got (though don't try to add more than an amount of liquid equal to what you started out with), reseason, decide if you can get away with a thinner sauce, and then thicken if you must. Consider using something more substantial than water for your thinning: consommé or bouillon (be careful with the salt when you reseason), liquid from a compatible cooked vegetable you're serving with the meal, or even orange juice for something like ham or fowl-based dishes. To avoid slowing everything down, have your liquid hot before adding it.

Cream sauces can be extended by adding more white sauce (see your other cookbooks for a medium white sauce recipe) or even cream of mushroom or chicken soups if you're really strapped for time.

Hollandaise-based sauces are best left in their original, rich, unadulterated state. Serve the portions in the kitchen, and dollop the sauce on yourself. Nobody will even think to question the amount.

Not rich enough

Add heavy cream, 1 teaspoon at a time, after all the sauce is cooked and removed from the heat. A lump of butter, applied in like manner, will also work.

Salty

Add a couple of pinches of brown sugar. It tends to overcome saltiness without adding noticeable sweetening.

Separating: see SAUCES, *Curdled*

Too thin

There are almost as many thickeners as there are sauces. The universal one is time: Keep cooking until some liquid evaporates, and the sauce will thicken. (Some French recipes require sauce ingredients to be reduced by 90 per cent or more, and many a chef has been called on the carpet by unknowledgeable managers to explain, for instance, why it required 19 prize salmon to make one cup of *sauce béchamel.*)

Cornstarch is a good thickener when translucency of sauce is desirable, as in many dessert or Chinese sauces. Add 1 tablespoon per 1½ to 2 cups of cooking liquid. To prevent lumps, dissolve the cornstarch in cold water, then add to the hot sauce.

Arrowroot: 2½ tablespoons per 1½ to 2 cups, but only when the sauce will be served within 10 minutes. To prevent lumps, dissolve the arrowroot in cold water, then add to the hot sauce.

One cup of milk or a milk-based sauce will be thickened by 4 tablespoons of flour, 1 cup of bread crumbs, 3 to 4 tablespoons of tapioca, or 2 egg yolks beaten with ¼ cup of cream or evaporated milk. The latter should be done only in the top of a double boiler, stirring constantly.

Other sauce thickeners that may be appropriate for your particular sauce are rice, barley, milk, cream, and mashed-potato flakes.

SAUSAGES

Bursting, splitting, exploding, etc.

There are two schools of thought: the Low Temperaturists and the Skin Piercers. Either is likely to work; both are unnecessary. Next time cook the sausages using just enough water to cover, and if you are using the precooked variety (almost all are), use hot but not boiling water.

SCALLIONS: see ONIONS

SEA FOOD: see FISH AND SEA FOOD

SHORTENING: see FAT, LARD, SHORTENING

SHRIMP: see FISH AND SEA FOOD

SODA POP

Decarbonated

Cover tightly and shake well; some of the carbonization will be restored if it isn't too far gone. Open carefully; the soda may shoot across the room if you do it too fast.

SOUP STOCK

Have none, need some

Two bouillon cubes (beef or chicken) in a cup of water make an acceptable substitute for beef or chicken stock. Watch your salt levels, since bouillon is saltier than stock.

SOUPS

Bland

Chicken extract or bouillon will beef (or chicken) up a pallid soup. Beef extract or bouillon will do the same. So will yeast extract. Here is a list of common herbs and spices and their most exemplary uses in soups:

Allspice (whole): pea, ham, vegetable, beef, and tomato soups.

Basil: tomato, turtle, spinach, and minestrone soups (½ teaspoon per 4 servings).

Bay leaf: vegetable, minestrone, and tomato soups.

Chervil: tomato and spinach soups.

Cumin: a dash in creamed chicken, fish, and pea soups.

Juniper berries: 3 or 4 in 4 servings of vegetable, beef, lamb, or oxtail soups.

Mace: 1 or 2 blades (or pinches, if it's ground) in 4 cups of consommé stock.

Marjoram: spinach, clam, turtle, and onion soups (⅛ teaspoon per serving).

Oregano: tomato, bean, corn, and pea soups (add 5 minutes before serving).

Rosemary: chicken, pea, spinach, potato, and fish soups.

Sage: creamed soups and chowders.

Savory: fish, consommé, lentil, bean, tomato, and vegetable soups.

Sesame: creamed soups (sprinkle on before serving).

Tarragon: tomato, vegetable, and sea food soups.

Thyme: chicken, onion, potato, tomato, and sea food soups, gumbo, borsch (stir in ½ teaspoon 10 minutes before serving).

Bouillon cloudy

Add eggshells. Please remove them before serving.

Cold

Reheat thin soups in a heavy saucepan, a Dutch oven, or a deep skillet over a very low flame just to the boiling point.

Reheat thick soups in a deep casserole in a 375° oven until hot, stirring occasionally.

Consommé won't jell

This happens most often to canned consommé that has been around for a long time. The general rule for any consommé is that 1 tablespoon of gelatin powder will solidify 2 cups of consommé.

Fatty or greasy

If you have the time, refrigerate the soup. The fat will solidify on the top. Remove it and reheat (see SOUPS, *Cold*).

If you don't have the time, you can slurp up the fat from the top with a baster, or you can float a grease collector on the top. Lettuce leaves, blotting paper, and paper towels all make good grease collectors.

Another fast technique is to make a "grease magnet" by wrapping a few ice cubes in a terry-cloth towel. Run this over the top of the soup, and the fat will cling to it. A ladle full of ice cubes will have the same effect.

Light

There are commercial soup colorings, but some people think they have a telltale aroma. Depending on the kind of soup, you can darken it either with tomato skins or with a mixture of 1 teaspoon ground cinnamon, ½ teaspoon cloves, and ¼ teaspoon allspice dissolved in a cup of soup and added to each 2 quarts of liquid just before serving.

Salty

The surest solution is to increase the quantity of liquid without increasing the quantity of salt.

If this isn't practical, try one of the following three techniques.

1. Tomatoes: If it is the right kind of soup, add a can of tomatoes. They are sufficiently bland to use up a lot of the saltiness.

2. A couple of pinches of brown sugar: It won't desalt the soup, but it may help cover up the salty taste without sweetening the soup.

3. Potatoes: Add a thin-sliced raw potato, and keep it in the soup until the slices become translucent; they may absorb some of the salt from the liquid.

There are some skeptics who ask, "If it is possible to remove salt from liquid easily, why aren't we desalting the oceans?" To this we reply, "Because it would take 488,391,000,000,000 tons of sliced potatoes."

Too much

Contrary to almost everyone else's opinion, leftover soup can be kept almost indefinitely without freezing, if you're willing to work at it. Almost any soup will keep in a covered pot in the refrigerator for a week. If you have a great soup that you want to keep longer but don't want to freeze, take it out of the refrigerator and heat it to boiling every couple of days, and it should last for a year.

Too thin

First see the section on SAUCES, *Too thin,* for several useful hints. Thickeners peculiar to soups include these:

Mashed potatoes or potato flakes (which also have a tendency to absorb seasonings, so check for taste after adding).

Some of the soup's ingredients (*e.g.,* meat, vegetables) ground up in a blender and added. (These should be additional ingredients but, in a pinch, may be filched from the soup.)

A mixture of ½ cup cornstarch and ¼ cup sherry, stirred in shortly before serving.

One teaspoon of barley or rice or 2 teaspoons of flour for each original cup of liquid, stirred in during last hour of cooking.

One egg yolk beaten with 1 tablespoon of cream or sherry, mixed with a small amount of hot soup, and then stirred into the rest just before serving.

Stale bread (especially if you can float a heaping tablespoon of Parmesan cheese on top, too).

For long-cooking soups, a handful of oatmeal.

For pea and bean soups, 1 teaspoon of vinegar. (It will thicken without affecting the taste.)

SOUR CREAM

Have none, need some

For cooking purposes, not topping purposes, add 1 tablespoon of mild vinegar or lemon juice to 1 cup of evaporated milk.

For topping purposes, not cooking purposes, put cottage

cheese in the blender, sweeten it to taste, and if it doesn't taste right, add a bit of vanilla.

SPAGHETTI: see PASTA

SPAGHETTI SAUCE: see SAUCES

SPINACH: see GREENS

SQUASH, SWEET POTATOES, PUMPKIN

Bland

Squash, unbeknownst to many gastronomes, has a luscious affinity for ginger. To demonstrate this to yourself, serve squash of almost any sort with a heaping tablespoon of ginger marmalade per serving.

If this doesn't suit your fancy, try basil, ground cloves, dillseed, dill weed, mace, marjoram, oregano, sage, and thyme.

Not enough

The orange-colored squashes have a natural affinity for fruits, so combine chunks, or even purées, of them with sautéed apples or pears or sections of mandarin or regular oranges.

Green and yellow squashes love tomatoes and onions.

Stringy

Beat stringy squash with an electric mixer at high speed for 10 seconds, then at low speed for 60 seconds. Wash the strings off the beater (the floor, the walls, the dog), and repeat if necessary or possible.

Too much
Squash keeps better than almost any other vegetable; don't worry.

STEAK

Curling
Cut through the fat along the edge of the meat every inch or so.

Overdone
Continue cooking it until it is completely charred, and use it to scratch pictures on the walls of your cave.

Or how about covering your mistake (and the steak) with:

Hot Uruguayan Steak Sauce
Sauté ⅔ cup chopped onions and ⅓ cup chopped green peppers in 2 tablespoons olive oil for 5 minutes. Add ⅔ cup tomatoes (diced), 1 teaspoon salt, ⅛ teaspoon chili peppers, and ⅔ teaspoon paprika. Sauté 5 minutes. Mix in ⅔ cup peanuts (ground) and 1 cup chicken broth. Simmer 30 minutes. Stir in ¼ cup sour (or heavy) cream. Pour over steak (enough for about 2 pounds of steak) and serve.

Tough

If you don't have or would rather not use tenderizer, and if perforating the steak with a fork every ¼ inch doesn't appeal, try pounding it all over with the edge of a metal pie plate. Very effective, especially if you remove the pie first.

STEW

Bland

No stew has ever been made that couldn't be perked up by adding 4 tablespoons of sherry and stirring well just before serving. (If you think you've made one that couldn't be so improved, we'd like to see it. Smear some on a post card and send it, in care of the publisher.)

Burned

Transfer the unstuck part, without scraping, to another pot at once. A wooden spoon is best. Add more water if necessary. Add some more onions to the stew; they tend to overcome any burned flavor that may remain.

Falling apart

Sometimes stew just cooks itself to bits. You can't reassemble it, so serve it over noodles or rice; it will look like a great sauce.

Fatty

If the consistency permits, the fat may be skimmed off with a paper towel.

If it doesn't, chill the stew after it is fully cooked, remove the solidified fat, and return to the pot. Most stews taste better the next day anyway.

Not enough

Serve the stew over noodles. Add more vegetables—and don't forget that beans are protein food. A can of kidney or Lima beans can stretch a stew without thinning it out.

Salty

Increase the quantity without adding more salt if at all pos-

sible. If not, add a couple of pinches of brown sugar; it tends
to mask the saltiness without adding any sweetness.

Too thin
The best thickener for most stews is a handful of mashed-potato
flakes stirred in. (See soups, *Too thin,* for additional suggestions.)

Tough
A teaspoon of sugar in the stewpot will help make tough stew
meat grow tender much faster. The acid in tomatoes has the
same effect, so add some fresh or canned tomatoes if they will
be compatible.

STRAWBERRIES: see berries

STRING BEANS: see beans, lima and string

STUFFING
Bland
Add allspice, basil, a crushed bay leaf, coriander, ginger,
marjoram, oregano, sage, savory, and/or thyme.

Or perhaps the stuffing could use diced celery, chopped chestnuts or walnuts, diced onions (browned or not), or sausage or
bacon, browned and crumbled in.

SUGAR
Hard, lumpy, solidified
Here are six things to do with hardened or lumpy sugar—the
least drastic first, and so on, up to the last resort.

1. Push it through a sieve.
2. Roll it out with a rolling pin.
3. Steam it in the top of a double boiler.
4. Put it, in its bag (not box), in a 350° oven. By the time
the bag is warm, the sugar should be softened or delumped.
5. Put it through a meat grinder or blender.
6. Give up and melt it down over slow heat on the stove; it

makes good syrup. Add extracts, like vanilla, maple, or butter-scotch.

To keep sugar from going hard or lumpy in the future, especially brown sugar, keep it in an airtight jar, preferably in the refrigerator. To be doubly sure, keep a piece of apple or lemon in the jar.

Have none, need some
In cooking, the following may be substituted for 1 cup of sugar (don't forget to reduce the amount of other liquids in the recipe where appropriate): ¾ cup honey, 1½ cups molasses, 2 cups corn syrup, or 1½ cups maple syrup.

Also bear in mind that you can make superfine sugar out of regular granulated sugar, in your blender.

SWEET POTATOES: see SQUASH, SWEET POTATOES, PUMPKIN

SWISS CHARD: see GREENS

SYRUP
Crystallized
Heat it gently, and the crystals should go away. Probably the simplest way is by standing the syrup jug in a bowl of hot water.

TEA
Cloudy
For hot tea, put a couple of lemon slices in the pitcher or pot. For iced tea, add a small dash of boiling water.

TOMATO SOUP: see SOUPS

TOMATOES
Acidy
Canned tomatoes sometimes get unpleasantly acidy in taste. Add 1 teaspoon of sugar to a 2-pound-or-so can to combat this.

Bland

Cooked tomatoes go nicely with basil, celery seed, ground cloves, oregano, or sage.

Green

Green tomatoes will ripen off the vine when wrapped in newspaper and stored in a cool place. They will ripen fairly slowly, however—at least 4 to 5 days from green to red. Wouldn't you rather make tomato pickles (see your cookbook) or perhaps:

Denise Krause's Southern Fried Tomatoes

Slice green tomatoes into thick slices. Sprinkle with salt and pepper. Dip in a mixture of ½ cup corn meal, ½ teaspoon thyme, and 1 tablespoon brown sugar. Fry in butter until brown. Especially good with lamb.

Hard to peel

Pour boiling water over the tomatoes and let sit for 3 minutes. Or hold them over an open flame, skewered on a long fork, until the skin breaks. This heat treatment is permanent, so you can boil now and peel later if it suits your purpose.

If you don't want to heat the tomatoes at all, try stroking the skin with the dull edge of a kitchen knife until all the skin is wrinkled. It should come off easily at this juncture. (If it doesn't, perhaps you are at the wrong juncture.)

Old

When your fresh tomatoes are getting on in days, try turning them over. Tomatoes will keep longer when stored stem side down.

Too many

You can use tomatoes in dozens of ways at every meal, from tomato omelets for breakfast to homemade Bloody Marys for a nightcap (put 1 tomato, 1 shot of vodka, and 1 dash of Worcestershire in a blender; blend at high speed for 1 minute). The only important watchword is that tomatoes should never be frozen.

TONGUE

Bland

There's not a whole lot you can do with a tongue. But you might add 4 or 5 whole allspices and/or some celery seed to the cooking water.

Hard to peel

Add 1 tablespoon of vinegar to the cooking water, and cook 10 minutes longer. Peel while the tongue is still hot.

TUNA FISH: see FISH AND SEA FOOD

TURKEY: see POULTRY

TURNIP GREENS: see GREENS

TURNIPS

Bland

So who ever heard of a lively turnip? You can try to liven yours up with either dillseed, dill weed, or poppy seed in the cooking water, and good luck to you.

Old

Old turnips will taste younger, and better, if you blanch them 5 minutes before cooking. To blanch a turnip, plunge it into a large-enough quantity of boiling water so that the boiling

doesn't stop. Leave it in 5 minutes, then proceed as you will. You can blanch your turnips in advance, dipping them in cold water after the 5 minutes to stop the cooking, and use them much later if you wish.

Smelly
Turnips will smell a lot less if you add 1 teaspoon of sugar to the cooking water.

VEAL

Bland
Consider the addition of these seasonings, all of which do something for veal: ground allspice, celery seed (sprinkle it on a roast), chervil, cloves (5 or 6 in the gravy), marjoram, oregano, paprika, rosemary, saffron, sage (rub the roast with it), or tarragon.

Not white (tender, succulent) enough
If you have the time, soak the veal in milk overnight in the refrigerator. If you don't have the time, blanch the veal briefly, starting with cold water.

VEGETABLE SOUP: see SOUPS

VEGETABLES: see specific vegetables

WAFFLES: see PANCAKES

WALNUTS: see NUTS

WELSH RABBIT: see CHEESE, *Rubbery, tough, stringy*

WHIPPED CHEAM

Hard to whip, won't whip
Chill the cream and the bowl and the beaters. If that doesn't work, add any of the following thickeners: 1 unbeaten egg white, 3 or 4 drops of lemon juice, a pinch of gelatin powder, or a bit of salt sprinkled in, and keep whipping.

Have none, need some

For most uses, you can substitute 1 mashed banana beaten up with 1 egg white (beat the egg white stiff first) and sugar to taste.

Overwhipped, separated

You'll never have whipped cream, but if you keep on going a bit longer, you'll have delicious homemade butter! Keep beating until it turns solid. Drain off the liquid. Refrigerate until it is hard. Knead it by hand to press out the liquid (which is whey, so now you know what it was L. M. Muffet was eating with her curds). Now you have sweet butter. If you want salt butter, add ¼ teaspoon salt per pint of cream that you started with, and knead some more.

WIENERS: see SAUSAGES

WINE

Cold

If the wine gets too cold, you'd better use it for cooking; there is no way to warm wine without the flavor being lost.

Sour

You can't desour wine, so let it keep on souring, and eventually you'll have some lovely wine vinegar.

ZEBRA

Actually we have no hints for cooking zebra; we just didn't want the book to end on a sour note.

hawed Frozen Foods

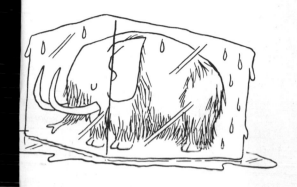

frozen foods, either intentionally or acci-
have no need for them right away, most
d that you do not refreeze; either store them
use them right away or throw them out.
you must now ask yourself is this: How
ng you otherwise would it take to get you
One? Ten? A hundred?
o you. We do, however, offer one reputable
at it is all right to refreeze thawed foods.
Maclinn, a research specialist in food tech-
versity.
is all right. He says you can expect the
softer than normal when they are thawed
herwise everything is all right.

Appendixes

Index

Recipes

T

When food bur
  1. Stop the f
  2. Separate
  3. Treat the
taste.
  Here is how
  1. Remove
tainer bigger
water, and p
of the essen
the cooking;
  2. Using
that don't
you don't
what come
is, see the
  3. Tast
now, but
stand for
pleasantl
—unless
barbecu
was.

When you defrost
dentally, and you
authorities recommen
in the refrigerator, or
  The basic question
many authorities tell
to change your mind?
  We leave this up t
authority who says th
He is Dr. Walter A.
nology at Rutgers Un
  Dr. Maclinn says i
foods to be somewhat
the second time, but o

Too Much Food; How to Store It

This chart gives you an idea of how long leftover foods can survive in the refrigerator and freezer. The times are only approximate, and we make no guarantees, because we don't know how old the food was when you bought it or how close to ideal temperatures your refrigerator performs. (Optimum temperatures are 0° in the freezer and 34° to 38° in the refrigerator.) We have tended to be conservative; in most cases, a little bit longer shouldn't hurt. In the Special Instructions column, (F) refers to freezer only and (R) to refrigerator only.

Kind of Food	Refrigerator	Freezer	Special Instructions
BREAD, CAKES, ROLLS	1–2 das.	2 mos.	
DAIRY PRODUCTS			
Butter, margarine	1–2 wks.	3 mos.	(F) Wrap tightly.
Cheese			
Cottage, ricotta	3–5 das.	2–3 mos.	Do not freeze creamed cottage cheese or cream cheese. (F) Wrap tightly; cheese may become crumbly.
Other soft cheeses	1–2 wks.	2–3 mos.	
Hard cheeses	3–6 mos.	6 mos.	
Ice cream	2 das.	1 mo.	
Milk, cream	3 das.	Do not freeze	

Kind of Food	Refrigerator	Freezer	Special Instructions
EGGS			
Yolks or whites, separated, raw	1–2 das.	6–8 mos.	(ʀ) Keep yolks covered with water; whites in covered containers. (ꜰ) Do not freeze in shells. Break eggs into container; separate yolks and whites if desired. Cover container tightly.
Whole, raw	7 das.	6–8 mos.	
Hard-boiled	8–10 das.	Do not freeze	
FISH			
Cod, flounder, haddock, halibut, shrimp	1 da.	4 mos.	(ʀ) Wrap or cover loosely. (ꜰ) Wrap tightly in freezer wrap and tape well. Use wax paper to separate individual pieces.
Mullet, ocean perch, sea trout, striped bass, shucked clams	1 da.	3 mos.	
Salmon, crab meat	1 da.	2 mos.	
Cooked fish, shellfish	1–2 das.	3 mos.	
FRUITS			
Citrus fruits, apples	7 das.	Do not freeze	(ʀ) Store uncovered or in crisper section. (ꜰ) Fruits other than whole berries should be packed in sugar or syrup plus ascorbic acid (vitamin C).
Fruit-juice concentrates	6 das.	12 mos.	
All other fruits	3–5 das.	10–12 mos.	
MEATS			
Beef, roasts, steaks	3–5 das.	12 mos.	(ʀ) Wrap or cover loosely. (ꜰ) Wrap tightly in freezer wrap and tape well. Use wax paper to separate individual pieces.
Cooked meat (all kinds)	1–2 das.	3 mos.	
Ground meat	1–3 das.	1–3 mos.	

Kind of Food	Refrigerator	Freezer	Special Instructions
Lamb			
Chops	2–3 das.	6–7 mos.	
Roasts	5–6 das.	6–7 mos.	
Liver, kidneys,			
tongue	1–2 das.	1–3 mos.	
Pork, cured			
Bacon	7 das.	2–3 mos.	
Frankfurters	7 das.	1 mo.	
Ham, sliced	3–5 das.	1–2 mos.	
Ham, whole	7 das.	1–2 mos.	
Pork, fresh	3–5 das.	8 mos.	
Veal, all kinds	3–5 das.	6–8 mos.	
POULTRY			
Chicken, cooked	1–2 das.	6 mos.	(R) Wrap or cover
Chicken, pieces	1–2 das.	6 mos.	loosely. (F) Wrap
Chicken, whole	1–2 das.	12 mos.	solid pieces tightly in
Chicken livers	1–2 das.	3 mos.	freezer wrap and tape
All other poultry			well. Put cooked juicy
(goose, turkey,			dishes in tightly closed,
duck, etc.)	1–2 das.	6 mos.	rigid containers.
SOUPS, STEWS,			(R) See special hint
CASSEROLES	1–2 das.	2 mos.	under soups, *Too*
			much.
VEGETABLES			
Canned (open);			(R) Store canned
cooked	1–3 das.	8–10 mos.	(open) or cooked vege-
Fresh, aboveground	3–5 das.	8–10 mos.	tables in covered con-
Fresh, root	1–2 wks.	8–10 mos.	tainer. Store fresh
			vegetables uncovered
			or in crisper section.
			(F) Boil or blanch
			before freezing. Do
			not freeze tomatoes,
			radishes, or any very
			crisp vegetables.

135

Seasonability of Fruits and Vegetables

The simple fact is that fresh fruits and vegetables bought at the peak of their seasons taste an awful lot better than at other times. With modern hothouse and storage techniques, many items are available at the market for much longer periods than they used to be, but they are still best in peak season. The following chart shows you just when those peak seasons are. A = available; P = peak season; − = not available.

Fruits	Jan	Feb	Mar	Apr	May	June	July	Aug	Sept	Oct	Nov	Dec
Apples	A	A	A	A	A	A	A	A	P	P	P	P
Apricots	−	−	−	−	A	P	P	A	−	−	−	−
Avocados	A	A	P	P	A	A	A	A	A	A	A	A
Bananas	A	A	P	P	P	P	A	A	A	A	A	A
Blackberries	−	−	−	−	A	P	P	P	−	−	−	−
Blueberries	−	−	−	−	A	A	P	P	A	−	−	−

136

Fruits	Jan	Feb	Mar	Apr	May	June	July	Aug	Sept	Oct	Nov	Dec
Cherries	—	—	—	—	A	P	P	A	—	—	—	—
Cranberries	A	—	—	—	—	—	—	—	A	P	P	A
Grapefruit	P	P	P	P	A	A	A	A	A	A	P	P
Grapes	A	A	A	A	A	A	A	A	P	P	P	A
Lemons	A	A	A	A	A	P	P	A	A	A	A	A
Limes	A	A	A	A	A	P	P	P	A	A	A	A
Melons	—	A	A	A	A	A	P	P	P	P	A	A
Oranges	P	P	P	A	A	A	A	A	A	A	A	P
Peaches	—	—	—	—	—	A	P	P	A	—	—	—
Pears	A	A	A	A	A	A	A	P	P	P	A	A
Persimmons	—	—			—	—	—	A	A	P	P	A
Pineapples	A	A	P	P	P	P	A	A	A	A	A	A
Quinces	P	A	—	—	—	—	—	—	A	P	P	P
Raspberries	—	—	—	—	A	P	A	A	A	A	—	—
Rhubarb	A	A	A	P	P	P	A	A	A	A	A	A
Strawberries	A	A	A	A	P	P	A	A	A	A	A	A
Tangerines	P	A	A	A	—	—	—	—	—	—	A	P
Watermelons	—	—	—	A	A	P	P	A	A	—	—	—

Vegetables

	Jan	Feb	Mar	Apr	May	June	July	Aug	Sept	Oct	Nov	Dec
Artichokes	A	A	P	P	A	—	—	—	—	A	A	A
Asparagus	—	—	A	P	P	P	—	—	—	—	—	—
Beets, greens	A	A	P	P	A	A	A	A	—	—	A	A
Broccoli	P	P	P	A	A	A	A	A	A	P	P	P
Brussels sprouts	A	A	A	—	—	—	—	A	A	P	P	P
Cabbage	A	A	A	A	P	A	A	A	A	A	A	A
Carrots	P	P	P	P	P	P	P	P	P	P	P	P
Cauliflower	A	A	A	A	A	A	A	A	A	P	P	A
Celery	P	P	P	P	P	P	P	P	P	P	P	P
Chard	A	A	A	A	A	A	P	P	P	P	A	A
Chicory	A	A	A	A	A	P	A	A	A	A	A	A

137

Vegetables	Jan	Feb	Mar	Apr	May	June	July	Aug	Sept	Oct	Nov	Dec
Collards	P	A	A	A	A	A	A	A	A	A	A	P
Corn	A	A	A	A	A	P	P	P	P	A	A	A
Cucumbers	A	A	A	A	P	P	P	P	A	A	A	A
Dandelion greens	A	A	P	P	P	P	A	A	A	A	A	A
Eggplant	A	A	A	A	A	A	A	P	P	A	A	A
Endive	P	P	P	A	A	A	A	A	A	A	A	P
Escarole	A	A	A	A	A	A	A	A	A	P	A	A
Green beans	A	A	A	A	P	P	P	P	A	A	A	A
Green peppers	A	A	A	A	A	A	P	P	P	P	A	A
Kale	P	P	A	A	A	A	A	A	A	A	A	P
Lettuce	A	A	A	A	A	P	A	A	A	A	A	A
Lima beans	A	—	A	A	A	A	P	P	P	P	A	A
Mushrooms	A	A	A	A	A	A	A	A	A	A	P	P
Mustard greens	A	A	A	A	A	P	P	A	A	A	A	A
Okra	A	A	A	A	A	P	P	A	A	A	A	A
Onions, Bermuda	A	A	P	P	P	P	A	A	A	A	A	A
Onions, green	A	A	A	A	P	P	P	P	A	A	A	A
Parsnips	P	P	P	P	P	P	P	P	P	P	P	P
Potatoes	P	P	P	P	P	P	P	P	P	P	P	P
Pumpkins	—	—	—	—	—	—	—	—	A	P	A	—
Radishes	A	A	A	P	P	P	P	A	A	A	A	A
Rutabagas	P	P	P	A	A	A	A	A	A	P	P	P
Spinach	A	A	P	P	P	P	A	A	A	A	A	A
Squash	—	—	—	—	—	—	—	—	A	P	A	—
Tomatoes	A	A	A	A	A	P	P	P	P	P	A	A
Turnips	P	P	P	A	A	A	A	A	A	P	P	P
Watercress	A	A	A	P	P	A	A	A	A	A	A	A
Wax beans	A	A	A	A	P	P	P	P	A	A	A	A

How to Measure and Pour Foods

THE ART OF MEASURING

When you are following other people's recipes, it is usually wise to use standard measuring spoons and cups, since that is what the recipe maker probably used. (There are exceptions. The story is told of the haughty couple who, having dined out, asked that the chef be presented to them. When he appeared, they asked him, cajoled him, perhaps even bribed him for the secret of his specialty dish. Finally he gave in. A pinch of this, a handful of that, and so on, he related, and finally, "Just before serving, add one mouthful of wine.")

When you measure dry ingredients (flour, sugar, etc.), heap the cup or spoon to overflowing and then level it off with something flat, like a knife blade or spatula.

When measuring sifted flour, always sift before measuring, and never pack the flour into the measuring cup or spoon; that will unsift it.

On the other hand, moist or dense ingredients, like butter and brown sugar, should be packed firmly into the measuring container.

Sticky ingredients (like honey and molasses) should be poured directly into the utensil; never try to dip the utensil into the container. If you grease the cup or spoon lightly, the sticky stuff won't stick.

WEIGHTS AND MEASURES YOU MAY NEED TO KNOW

A. Equivalent weights and measures

1 dash = about ⅛ teaspoon

1 teaspoon = ⅓ tablespoon

1 tablespoon = 3 teaspoons

2 tablespoons = ⅛ cup, or 1 ounce of liquid

4 tablespoons = ¼ cup

5⅓ tablespoons = ⅓ cup

8 tablespoons = ½ cup

16 tablespoons = 1 cup

1 cup = ½ pint of liquid

1 pint = 2 cups or 16 ounces of liquid

2 pints = 1 quart

4 quarts = 1 gallon

1 pound = 16 ounces

1 jigger of liquid = 1½ ounces = 3 tablespoons of liquid

B. How much of what weighs how much

Bread crumbs: 1 cup = 4 ounces
Butter: 1 stick = 4 ounces = ½ cup *
Butter: 2 cups = 1 pound = 4 sticks
Butter: 1 level tablespoon = ½ ounce
Flour: 1 level tablespoon = ½ ounce
Rice: 1 cup = 8 ounces
Sugar: 1 cup granulated = 8 ounces
Sugar: 1 cup brown = 6⅓ ounces
Sugar: 1 cup confectioners' = 5⅓ ounces

C. Can sizes

6-ounce can = 6 ounces = ¾ cup
8-ounce can = 8 ounces = 1 cup
No. 1 can = 11 ounces = 1⅓ cups
12-ounce can = 12 ounces = 1½ cups
No. 303 can = 16 ounces = 2 cups
No. 2 can = 20 ounces = 2½ cups
No. 2½ can = 28 ounces = 3½ cups

HOW TO POUR

Pouring ingredients from one utensil to another is such a simple thing, and yet it so often results in sugar or oil or milk or whatever all over the counter or floor.

The main thing you need to know about pouring is funnels. Not necessarily store-bought, fancy plastic or metal funnels, although those are all right, too. But homemade spur-of-the-moment funnels. For example, you carry one around with you all the time:

* 1 tablespoon = ⅝ inch of a stick. If you can't find a ruler, use the seam allowance of your dress. A standard seam is ⅝ inch wide.

your hand. It takes only a minute of practice to shape your hand into a funnellike shape, through which you can pour liquids or powders.

Or use paper. Almost any kind of paper, except paper towels, can be rolled up into a temporary funnel—even for liquids. You can pour a whole gallon of liquid through a funnel made from a piece of ordinary writing paper before it starts to get soggy. Consider, too, wax paper and aluminum foil.

Here are two laboratory tricks known to all chemists:

To pour powders very accurately from a jar, use a rotating, instead of a pouring, motion. Slant the jar or box slightly downward so the contents just fail to come out. Now rotate the jar or box back and forth, from left to right, and you will find you have amazingly accurate control over how much comes out.

To pour liquids from a large unwieldy can, where the hole or spout is not centered (as with big cans of oil, for example), pour with the spout at the *top*—that is, as far as possible from the container you are pouring into. This results in a steadier flow, less dripping, and a neater "cutoff" when you stop pouring.

A "Last-Resort" Dinner

Here is a quite satisfactory meal for 4 persons, made up entirely of items on the "first-aid" list given on page 12. It should take about 20 to 25 minutes from the time you discover your regular dinner is ruined until you sit down at the table.

MENU

Beef in Sherried Cheese Sauce on Biscuits
Asparagus
Poached Pears in Vanilla Pudding with Whipped Topping

First heat the oven to the temperature given on the biscuit-mix box. While the oven is heating, toss a bowl (not plastic) and your beaters (whether electric or hand) into the freezer. Open the can of pears, and place ½ cup of the juice in the freezer for later.

Now make the biscuit dough following the recipe on the box. Don't bother to roll out perfect rounds the way it says, however; they'll be buried under cheese anyway. Instead, divide the dough into heaps (2 per person), and flatten them out gently until ½ inch thick, on a greased cooky sheet. Put them in the oven.

While the biscuits are baking, put the cheese sauce or soup in a saucepan over low heat, and add ¼ cup of milk (which you have made from your powdered milk if you have no fresh). Then start separating the chipped beef from two jars into a large strainer or colander. Rinse the beef under gently running hot water, turning it over once or twice, for about 1 minute. Drain, pat dry between paper towels, and drop in the cheese sauce. Add 1 tablespoon of sherry, and stir once. (This may not seem like enough meat, but, remarkably, 2 ounces of beef per person should suffice.)

Now start warming the asparagus. (If you wish, you can warm up the hollandaise for the asparagus, but we tend to think that would make too many sauces and too mushy a meal.)

Now start making the pears. Place the drained pears in a saucepan. Mix up the instant vanilla pudding, using ½ cup less milk than the instructions on the box call for.* Add 2 tablespoons of sherry to the pudding, pour it over the pears, and begin warming over very low heat.

By now the biscuits are ready, so top them with the meat and sauce and serve, along with the asparagus.

You'll have to get up after a few minutes to turn off the pears —they should cook about 10 minutes in all.

After the main course, make the topping by whipping together ½ cup of powdered milk with the pear juice you put in the freezer, until soft peaks form (3 to 4 minutes). Add 2 tablespoons of lemon juice, and beat until stiff (about another 3 to 4 minutes). If you have some, fold in ¼ cup of sugar. Spoon the topping onto the pear-pudding mix (which you have put in individual bowls), and serve the dessert at once.

* Most instant puddings can be made by beating or shaking. If you need to beat yours, don't forget your beater is in the freezer. Rinse and put it back as soon as you're done with it.

Stains

Here are suggestions on how to remove the most common food and food-related stains. On colored fabrics, it is always safest to treat an inconspicuous area with the cleaning solution before removing the entire stain.

Alcoholic beverages: Sponge with amyl acetate (banana oil) or cleaning fluid. Launder in hot water, and rinse in warm water.

Blood: Soak in cold water. Wash in warm water. If stain remains, soak in ammonia water (2 tablespoons per gallon).

Chocolate, cocoa: Soak in cold water; sponge in hot sudsy water. Bleach with hydrogen peroxide if necessary. Wash in hot water (warm for colored fabrics).

Coffee, tea: Pour boiling water through stain. Launder normally. If stain remains, bleach with hydrogen peroxide.

Egg: Soak in cold water; never hot. Launder normally with hot water. For colored fabrics, if color fast, soak in solution of 2 tablespoons detergent and 1 tablespoon hydrogen peroxide per gallon of water. Launder normally with warm water.

Fruits: Rinse in cold running water; wash in hot water with detergent. If stain remains, bleach with hydrogen peroxide.

Lipstick: Rub with lard, and blot until no more color is transferred to blotter. Wash in hot water (warm for colored fabrics) with detergent. Bleach with hydrogen peroxide if necessary.

Meat, gravy: Soak in cold water; never hot. Wash with hot water (warm for colored fabrics) and detergent. Bleach with hydrogen peroxide if necessary.

Milk, cream, ice cream: Rinse under cold running water. Wash in hot water (warm for colored fabrics) with detergent.

Mustard: Work glycerin in; rub spot; then wash in hot water (warm for colored fabrics) with detergent. If stain remains, bleach with hydrogen peroxide.

Soft drinks: Sponge with equal parts of alcohol and glycerin, or with lukewarm water and alcohol. Launder in hot water (warm for colored fabrics) and detergent.

Vegetables: Rinse in cold running water. Wash in hot water with detergent (warm for colored fabrics). If stain remains, bleach with hydrogen peroxide.

Problems with Utensils

Look first for the kind of problem, like *Burned* or *Clogged*, and then for the kind of utensil, like pot or meat grinder.

Burned
For aluminum, iron, ceramic, Pyrex, and stainless pots and pans, first scrape out what you can with a wooden spoon. (Alternate method: Add lots of salt to the contents, and heat on the stove; the food may "flake" out along with the salt.)

Then partly fill with water and a strong detergent. Boil for 10 minutes. Let stand as is overnight. Then pour off the water, and the burned part will be cleanable with a scouring pad or steel wool.

For aluminum pans, the following miracle can often be worked: Boil an onion in the pan, and the burned stuff will detach itself and rise to the top.

If a truly beloved utensil is "hopelessly" burned, there are professionals who specialize in restoring such items. They clean them with strong acid and repolish the metal. This will cost more than buying a new one, but if it was the pot you cooked the goulash in that caused Harry to propose to you, it may be worth it. Check the Yellow Pages under "Metal Finishers."

Clogged coffee strainer
Sprinkle coarse salt in the basket, and run under hot water.

Clogged meat grinder
Insert crumpled wax paper after the food, and keep grinding away.

The paper will force every last bit of food through but won't go through itself or jam up the works.

Cracked dishes or plates
For hairline cracks, put the plate in a pan of milk and boil for 45 minutes. The crack will usually disappear; if not, it was probably bigger than you thought.

Dirty aluminumware
Boil apple peels in aluminum pots; it will make cleaning them (the pots) ever so much easier. Something chemical, you know.

Dirty bottles
If the bottle brush won't reach or isn't strong enough, fill the bottle halfway with soapy water, and add a handful of pea-sized pebbles. Shake vigorously. Save the pebbles for another time.

Dirty enamelware
Fill with cold water plus 3 tablespoons of salt. Let sit overnight. Then boil. Then empty. Then clean (easily).

Dirty forks
Try cleaning them with an old toothbrush. (Dirty toothbrush? Try cleaning it with an old fork.)

Dirty grinder
Run a piece of bread through it before you wash it.

Dirty oven
Sprinkle salt on any spillovers that occur while baking. When the oven cools, you should be able to use a spatula to lift up the boilover in one big ugly piece.

Dirty pots and pans
Some kinds of dirt are best cleaned in cold water, not hot. These include eggs, doughs, sauces, and puddings.

Dirty Thermos bottles
Fill with warm water plus 1 heaping teaspoon of baking soda. Let sit overnight; then clean.

Drippy pitcher
If you're sure someone hasn't given you one of those dribble pitchers from the joke shop, you can quell drips by rubbing the tip of the lip of the pitcher with a tiny bit of butter. There's a tongue twister there somewhere, but we can't quite find it.

Dull scissors
Cut a piece of sandpaper into strips. You'll not only have a lovely collection of narrow strips of sandpaper; you'll have a sharper pair of scissors.

Greasy dishes, pots, pans
Hot-soak them with baking soda in the water. Chemically, baking soda plus grease equals soap. Not soap you'd use on the baby, but nevertheless soap that will clean your utensils.

Greasy ironware
Pour in lots of salt, and you can easily wipe up grease plus salt with paper towels.

Hands (your very own)

BURNED
Vanilla extract will help take away the initial pain; so will a paste of baking soda and water. So will a good stiff shot of bourbon.

GREASY
Very hot water will generally dissolve and remove most food-type grease. Next time, for greasing baking pans and the like, wear a wax-paper or plastic-wrap sandwich bag as a glove to smear the butter around with.

SMELLY
One of the finest household hints devised by man (are you listening, Heloise?) was announced by Hank Weaver on his commentary program on radio station KABC in Los Angeles in 1956. It went as follows: "Ladies, to get that ugly onion smell off your hands once and for all, simply rub them with garlic."

149

Slightly more reputable methods of deonionizing your hands are the following: (1) wash with cold water, rub hands with salt, and rinse; (2) rub hands with celery salt and wash normally; (3) rub with a raw, unpeeled potato; (4) wash with milk, then with cold water.

For fishy-odored hands, dampen them, rub with salt, wash normally, and then rub with a lemon rind. (If this doesn't work, have you considered the possibility that your hands just naturally smell like fish?)

STAINED

There are two ways to get off most fruit and some vegetable stains. One is to rub the stain with a raw potato, unpeeled, and then wash normally. The other, best with acid-fruit stains but good for many others as well, is to wash the hands, wipe lightly, strike a match, and cup your hands around the match to catch the smoke. Stains vanish as if by magic, leaving only the clean, blistered (if you keep them there too long) hands.

Rusting cake tins
Scour them with a hunk of raw potato dipped in cleaning powder.

Rusting ironware
Immerse in turpentine for anywhere from 1 hour to 3 days, de-

pending on how much rust. Then scour with steel wool. You'll have to break the ironware in all over again.

Rusting knives
Stick them through an onion for ½ hour, then wash and polish. Wipe them with a very light coating of vegetable oil to keep the rust from returning.

Smelly bottles
Fill bottle half full of water. Add 1 tablespoon of mustard or baking soda. Shake well, and let stand for 1 hour; then rinse.

Smelly cutting board
Rub it with a sliced lemon or lime.

Smelly dishes
Wash them in salty water. Or use a little ammonia in hot soapy water. Or add a bit of ground mustard to the wash water.

Smelly garbage disposal
Grind up half a lemon, orange, or grapefruit in it.

Smelly grater
Rub a hard crust of bread over it.

Smelly kitchen
For an inexpensive and delightful kitchen deodorizer, put some orange peel in the oven at 350°, with the door ajar.

Smelly pots and pans
Wash them in salt water or in hot soapy water plus a dash of ammonia.

Smoking griddle
This hint alone is worth the price of the book. This may be the most useful hint ever devised. This is the kind of hint that will make you want to drop everything and call up all your friends and relations and share it with them before another minute goes by. Are you ready? All right, here it is: To keep your griddle from smoking, rub it regularly with half a rutabaga. (Applause?)

Stained or darkened aluminumware

Rub it with half a rutabaga. No, sorry, we were just overcome with emotion from the last hint. Boil 2 teaspoons of cream of tartar in 1 quart of water for 10 minutes to lighten darkened aluminum.

Stained dishes

Soak them overnight in hot soda water (that's water plus baking soda). Then rub with a vinegar-moistened cloth dipped in salt. This is especially effective on tea stains.

Stained glassware

Go to your local repair shop and take them to the stained-glass window. If the stains are coffee stains, make tea in the utensil; the tannic acid of the tea should remove the coffee stains.

Stained plasticware

Soak for 20 minutes in a gallon of warm water plus 1 cup of bleach. Wipe dry and then wash normally.

If this doesn't work, rub the stains with dry baking soda.

If that doesn't work, sand the plastic with a very fine grade of silicon carbide paper (the black stuff that feels like sandpaper). Be sure the plastic is wet when you sand it.

Stained stainless steel

This is like giving instructions for ironing permanent-press fabrics. The rainbowlike stains are permanent; they will never come out. For brownish stains, soak a dishcloth in full-strength ammonia, cover the stain with it for 30 minutes, and wash normally.

Stained Teflon

In the utensil, boil a mixture of 1 cup water, ½ cup bleach, and 2 tablespoons baking soda. Then wash in warm suds. Recoat the Teflon with oil before using it.

Stuck bottle or jar tops

H. Allen Smith revealed to the world *the* technique for opening all screw-top containers. Now there are untold millions of us who face Mount Kisco or wherever it is he lives and say thank you every time we are faced with an obstinate top.

The technique: Bang the top *flatly* on a hard surface, like the floor. Not the edge, but the flat surface of the top. Just once. Hard. That's all. And to think of all those jars we used to hold under hot water.

Stuck plastic wrap
Some people, discouraged by the failure of the plastic-wrap people to come up with a product where you can find the end when you want it, have taken to keeping their plastic wrap in the refrigerator. It is the case that cold plastic wrap is easier to handle and just as effective.

Stuck-together glasses
Put cold water in the top one and put the bottom one in hot water, and they will come apart.

Worn-out woodenware
If it is really worth saving, here's how: Sand thoroughly. Then make a mixture of 1 tablespoon mineral oil and ½ tablespoon powdered pumice (from the hardware store). Rub on the wood with cheesecloth until it is dry and smooth—perhaps ½ hour. Let dry for 24 hours. Remove the dust. Repeat this operation 10 or 12 times, as necessary. Never, never wax, shellac, or polish a good wooden bowl.

Index

We like the next
have this face edition.
observed would of We
that be tradition have
all like and included
cookbooks putting leaving a
have an the listing
indexes index index of
at at off. the
the at If various
back. back this recipes
It of seriously that
seems the inconveniences appear
to dictionary you in
us or let the
however the us book
that telephone know so
putting book. and that
an So we'll you
index we tack can
on are one find
a flying on them
book in the again.

Recipes